U.S. Department of Justice
Office of Justice Programs

I0448841

July 2006, NCJ 214646

Bureau of Justice Statistics

Special Report

Prison Rape Elimination Act of 2003

Sexual Violence Reported by Correctional Authorities, 2005

By Allen J. Beck, Ph.D.
and Paige M. Harrison

BJS Statisticians

On September 4, 2003, President George W. Bush signed into law the Prison Rape Elimination Act of 2003 (P.L. 108-79). The legislation requires the Bureau of Justice Statistics (BJS) to develop new national data collections on the incidence and prevalence of sexual violence within correctional facilities. This report fulfills the requirement under Sec. 4 (c)(1) of the act for submission of an annual report on the activities of BJS with respect to prison rape.

In 2004, as one step in a multiphase implementation strategy, BJS completed the first-ever national survey of administrative records on sexual violence in adult and juvenile correctional facilities. In 2005 the survey was expanded to collect detailed information on substantiated incidents. New survey items included the circumstances surrounding each incident, characteristics of victims and perpetrators, the type of pressure or physical force, victim injuries, sanctions imposed, and victim assistance.

The 2005 survey results should not be used to rank systems or facilities. Future data collections, based on surveys of current and former inmates, are being developed to permit reliable comparisons of facilities.

Highlights

6,241 allegations of sexual violence in prison and jail reported in 2005, up from 5,386 in 2004

	2005	2004
Total*	6,241	5,386
Federal prisons	268	284
State prisons	4,341	3,172
Local jails	1,384	1,700
Private prisons/jails	204	210
Other facilities	44	20

*Based on adult correctional facilities only.

- 38% of allegations involved staff sexual misconduct; 35%, inmate-on-inmate nonconsensual sexual acts; 17%, staff sexual harassment; and 10%, inmate-on-inmate abusive sexual contact.

- There were 2.83 allegations of sexual violence per 1,000 inmates in 2005, up from 2.46 in 2004.

Correctional authorities substantiated 885 incidents of sexual violence in 2005, 15% of completed investigations

	Number of substantiated incidents	Rate per 1,000 inmates
Total*	885	0.40
Federal prisons	41	0.26
State prisons	458	0.39
Local jails	336	0.45
Private prisons/jails	37	0.31
Other facilities	13	1.21

*Estimates based on the reported number of substantiated incidents times the inverse probability of selection, and then summed.

- There were an estimated 0.40 substantiated incidents of sexual violence per 1,000 inmates in 2005, down from the 0.55 recorded in 2004.

- Based on completed investigations only, 37% of allegations of staff sexual misconduct in local jails and 15% in State prisons were substantiated.

Half of inmate-on-inmate sexual violence involved physical force or threat of force; two-thirds of staff misconduct was romantic

	Percent of substantiated inmate-on-inmate incidents	
	Nonconsensual	Abusive sexual contacts
Force/threat used	59%	33%
Victim injured	22	3
Victim given medical exam	63	33
Victim placed in protective custody	49	30
Perpetrator arrested/ prosecuted	58	39
Perpetrator placed in solitary confinement	72	70

- In prisons 67% of victims involved in staff sexual misconduct were male, while 62% of perpetrators were female. In jails 78% of victims of staff sexual misconduct were female; 87% of the perpetrators, male.

- Staff were arrested or prosecuted in 45% of substantiated incidents of staff sexual misconduct; discharged, fired or resigned in 82%.

Second administrative records collection conducted for 2005

Between January 1 and June 22, 2006, BJS completed the second national survey of the incidence and prevalence of sexual violence in correctional facilities. The Governments Division of the U.S. Census Bureau was the data collection agent for the survey. Initiated in 2004, the survey was conducted to provide information on occurrences of sexual violence based on allegations brought to the attention of correctional authorities. Although the results are limited to incidents reported to officials, the survey provides an understanding of what officials know, how many allegations were reported, and the outcomes of followup investigations.

In 2005 the survey was expanded to obtain data on each substantiated incident in which the event was investigated and determined to have occurred. Using a separate incident form, the survey obtained incident-based data on all substantiated allegations, providing a basis for an in-depth analysis of sexual violence. New information included details on the circumstances surrounding each incident, characteristics of victims and perpetrators, type of pressure or physical force used, victim injuries, sanctions imposed, and victim assistance.

Administrative records alone cannot provide reliable estimates of sexual violence. Due to fear of reprisal from perpetrators, a code of silence among inmates, personal embarrassment, and lack of trust in staff, victims are often reluctant to report incidents to correctional authorities.

BJS is developing and testing methods for more fully measuring the incidence of sexual violence in correctional facilities. These methods will rely on self-administered surveys to provide anonymity to victims when reporting their experiences. At the same time, computer-assisted technologies will ensure uniform conditions under which inmates complete the survey, and sampling techniques and supplemental data collections will reduce potential biases. (See box below for an update of these activities.)

Collection of victim self reports to begin in 2006

BJS is working toward full implementation of the Prison Rape Elimination Act. BJS has entered into cooperative agreements with —

1. Research Triangle International (RTI) (Raleigh, NC) to develop and test the adult prison and jail collection methodologies;
2. Westat, Inc. (Rockville, MD) to develop and test methodologies for measuring sexual violence in State and local juvenile facilities;
3. National Opinion Research Center (NORC) (Chicago, IL) to develop and test methods of collecting data from former inmates.

Though underlying survey methodology and logistical procedures differ with each of the data collection efforts, the measurement strategies will be consistent. The surveys will consist of an Audio Computer-Assisted Self-Interview (ACASI) in which respondents interact with a computer-administered questionnaire using a touch-screen and follow audio instructions delivered via headphones. The use of ACASI is expected to overcome many limitations of previous research. (See *Data Collections for the Prison Rape Elimination Act of 2003*, December 30, 2005.)

As of June 30, 2006, the following work had been completed or was underway:

Prison and jail inmates

• The ACASI questionnaire and survey protocols for adult inmates have been developed and tested. Between January and May 2006, BJS and RTI completed a pretest with more than 1,400 inmates in 4 State prisons, 4 local jail facilities, and 1 Federal prison. Results of the pretest will be published in October 2006 and assessed at a national meeting of stakeholders in November.

• In July 2006 BJS will submit an overview of all survey procedures, sampling methods, and questionnaires to the Office of Management and Budget (OMB) for approval to begin national implementation in late 2006.

• Procedures for selecting prison and jail facilities and for sampling inmates within selected facilities have been developed. In the first year of implementation, BJS expects to select 450 public and private prisons and jails and to interview more than 60,000 inmates.

• Upon OMB approval, RTI field staff will begin obtaining approval from State-level Institutional Review Boards (IRB) and begin interviews in January 2007.

Youth in residential placement facilities

• Survey procedures and questionnaires have been developed and reviewed by State and local administrators and other stakeholders. Cognitive testing of questionnaires with eligible youth began in June 2006.

• A formal pretest of collection methods in 10 juvenile facilities with up to 600 youth is planned for September 2006.

• National implementation is expected in 2007. Initial survey efforts will focus on more than 14,000 adjudicated youth in a sample of 150 State-operated facilities and 30 large, local or private facilities.

Former State prisoners

• An ACASI questionnaire, an administrative records form, and survey protocols have been developed to survey former inmates under active parole or post-custody supervision.

• A formal pretest of collection methods in 10-20 parole offices with up to 1,000 former inmates is planned for September 2006.

• National implementation is scheduled in 2007 with more than 11,500 completed interviews expected in 285 parole field offices.

The 2005 administrative survey provides the basis for the annual statistical review, as required under the act. These data will be used by the Review Panel on Prison Rape within the Department of Justice for purposes of conducting hearings concerning the operation of correctional facilities. The number of allegations and substantiated incidents for each system and sampled facility in the survey is provided. (See *Appendix tables.*)

2005 survey covered 1,867 adult correctional facilities

The 2005 survey included all Federal and State prison systems and facilities operated by the U.S. military and the Bureau of Immigration and Customs Enforcement (table 1). In addition, a representative sample was drawn of local jail jurisdictions, privately operated adult prisons and jails, and jails in Indian country. Altogether, the administrative survey covered 1,867 of the 5,220 adult facilities. These facilities housed more than 1.7 million inmates, or 78% of all inmates held in adult facilities in 2005.*

The survey was based on seven separate samples corresponding to the different types of facilities covered under the act. (See *Methodology,* page 11.) Each sample was designed in accordance with the requirement that BJS draw a random sample, or other scientifically appropriate sample, of not less than 10% of facilities. Entire systems were selected, when possible, to maximize reporting coverage. Local and private facilities were sampled to ensure at least one in each State and with selection probabilities proportionate to the number of inmates held.

In 2004 BJS developed uniform definitions of sexual violence. (See box to the left.) Incidents of inmate-on-inmate sexual violence were classified as *nonconsensual sexual acts* and *abusive sexual contacts.* Incidents of staff-on-inmate sexual violence were separated into *staff sexual misconduct* and *staff sexual harassment.* For purposes of this report, all such incidents are considered sexual violence.

---

*A survey of State-operated juvenile systems and privately or locally operated juvenile facilities was also conducted. Survey results for juvenile systems and facilities will be published in a separate report.

How sexual violence was measured

The definition of "rape" as required under the Prison Rape Elimination Act of 2003 was operationalized by disaggregating sexual violence into two categories of inmate-on-inmate sexual acts and two categories of staff sexual misconduct. The categories were —

Nonconsensual sexual acts

Contact of any person without his or her consent, or of a person who is unable to consent or refuse; and
• Contact between the penis and the vagina or the penis and the anus including penetration, however slight; or
• Contact between the mouth and the penis, vagina, or anus; or
• Penetration of the anal or genital opening of another person by a hand, finger, or other object.

Abusive sexual contacts

Contact of any person without his or her consent, or of a person who is unable to consent or refuse; and
• Intentional touching, either directly or through the clothing, of the genitalia, anus, groin, breast, inner thigh, or buttocks of any person.
• Excluding incidents in which the intent of the sexual contact is to harm or debilitate rather than sexually exploit.

Staff sexual misconduct

Any behavior or act of a sexual nature directed toward an inmate by an employee, volunteer, official visitor, or agency representative. Romantic relationships between staff and inmates are included. Consensual or nonconsensual sexual acts include:
• Intentional touching of the genitalia, anus, groin, breast, inner thigh, or buttocks with the intent to abuse, arouse, or gratify sexual desire; or
• Completed, attempted, threatened, or requested sexual acts; or
• Occurrences of indecent exposure, invasion of privacy, or staff voyeurism for sexual gratification.

Staff sexual harassment

Repeated verbal statements or comments of a sexual nature to an inmate by an employee, volunteer, official visitor, or agency representative, including:
• Demeaning references to gender or derogatory comments about body or clothing; or
• Profane or obscene language or gestures.

Table 1. Facilities selected for the Survey of Sexual Violence, 2005

Facility type	Number of facilities	Selected in the 2005 survey
Total	5,220	1,867
Prisons		
Public - Federal	84	All*
Public - State	1,320	All*
Private	319	31
Local jails		
Public	3,318	347
Private	38	5
Other adult facilities		
Indian country jails	68	7
Military-operated	59	All*
ICE-operated	14	All*

*The 2005 survey included all State prison systems, all Federal facilities, and all facilities operated by the U.S. military or the Bureau of Immigration and Customs Enforcement (ICE).

State prison reporting capabilities improve during 2005

The most serious forms of sexual violence (inmate-on-inmate nonconsensual sexual acts and staff sexual misconduct) were the most widely reported using survey definitions and reporting rules (table 2). During 2005 State and Federal prison authorities enhanced their abilities to report data on sexual violence.

Correctional authorities in more than 36 State and Federal prison systems were able to report incidents of inmate-on-inmate nonconsensual acts as defined in the 2005 survey (up from 34 in 2004). Authorities in 38 States were able to report incidents of abusive sexual contacts separately, while 10 combined these incidents with the more serious nonconsensual acts. Only 2 systems did not record abusive sexual contacts, down from 9 in 2004.

The greatest improvements in reporting were for staff sexual misconduct and harassment. In 2005 most prison administrators (44) were able to report data on staff sexual misconduct using survey definitions, up from 35 in 2004. Six systems were unable to separate sexual harassment from misconduct in 2005, down from nine in 2004. Only 1 system was unable to report any data on sexual harassment in 2005, down from 13 in 2004.

The ability to report incidents of sexual violence by authorities in sampled jail jurisdictions dropped during 2005. Also, jail authorities were less likely than prison authorities to meet survey definitions. A third of jail jurisdictions were unable to separate abusive sexual contacts from the more serious nonconsensual sexual acts; a fifth were unable to report staff sexual harassment separately from staff sexual misconduct.

The lower percents meeting survey requirements may be the result of the sampling procedures. More than two-thirds of the jail jurisdictions (242) received the definitions and reporting criteria for the first time in 2005, while all of the prison systems received the survey in 2004. BJS expects to work with administrators to improve reporting, especially in large jail jurisdictions with systems too large for manual searches of paper files.

As first noted in the 2004 report, the absence of uniform reporting necessitates caution when interpreting the survey results. The data should not be used to rank systems or facilities. Higher or lower counts, especially among jail jurisdictions, may reflect variations in definitions, reporting capacities, and procedures for recording allegations and not differences in the underlying incidence of sexual violence.

All selected correctional systems and facilities responded to the survey.

Sexual violence allegations increased

Reports of sexual violence varied across systems and sampled facilities, with every State prison system except New Mexico reporting at least one allegation of sexual violence. Among the 347 sampled local jails, 131 (38%) reported an allegation. About 42% of the 36 sampled privately operated prisons and jails reported at least one allegation.

Combined, the 2005 survey recorded 5,247 allegations of sexual violence. Taking into account weights for sampled facilities, the estimated total number of allegations for the Nation was 6,241. Expressed in terms of rates, there were 2.83 allegations of sexual violence per 1,000 inmates held in 2005, up from 2.43 per 1,000 inmates held in prisons, jails, and other adult correctional facilities in 2004. Prison systems reported 74% of all allegations; local jails, 22%; private prisons and jails, 3%; and other adult facilities, 1%.

Table 2. Reporting capabilities of correctional authorities to provide data on sexual violence, 2004 and 2005

Type of sexual violence	Federal and State prison systems		Local jails	
	2005	2004	2005	2004
Total	100.0%	100.0%	100.0%	100.0%
Nonconsensual sexual acts				
Full reporting	70.6%	66.7%	62.8%	78.0%
Partial*	9.8	7.8	2.3	7.4
Includes abusive sexual contacts	19.6	25.5	34.9	13.6
Unable to report	0	0	0	1.0
Abusive sexual contacts				
Full reporting	74.5%	51.0%	61.9%	84.9%
Partial*	0	5.9	0	0
Combined with other sexual acts	19.6	25.5	34.6	13.6
Unable to report	3.9	17.6	3.5	1.5
Staff sexual misconduct				
Full reporting	86.3%	68.6%	76.1%	88.4%
Partial*	2.0	5.9	1.4	2.5
Includes sexual harassment	13.7	17.6	21.3	7.9
Unable to report	0	7.8	1.2	1.2
Staff sexual harassment				
Full reporting	86.3%	52.9%	76.1%	90.3%
Partial*	0	3.9	0.3	0
Combined with sexual misconduct	11.7	17.6	21.9	7.9
Unable to report	2.0	25.5	1.7	1.7

*See *Appendix tables* for systems and facilities that reported only incidents that were completed or substantiated.

Nationwide, the number of allegations rose by nearly 16%. Consistent with improvements in reporting capabilities, State and Federal prison systems reported a 33% increase in the number of allegations; local jails reported a 19% decrease.

Allegations of sexual violence per 1,000 inmates, by type of facility, 2005

Facility type	National estimate	Rate per 1,000 inmates
Total	6,241	2.83
Prisons		
Public - Federal	268	1.71
Public - State	4,341	3.68
Private	182	1.80
Local jails		
Public	1,384	1.86
Private	22	1.33
Other adult facilities		
Indian country jails*	32	^
Military-operated	8	3.08
ICE-operated	4	0.60

*Excludes facilities housing juveniles only.
^Too few cases to provide a reliable rate.

About 38% of the reported allegations of sexual violence involved staff sexual misconduct, 35% involved inmate-on-inmate nonconsensual sexual acts; 17% staff sexual harassment; and 10% inmate-on-inmate abusive sexual contacts.

Allegations of sexual violence, by type of incident, 2005

Incident type	National estimate	Percent
Total	6,241	100.0 %
Inmate-on-inmate nonconsensual sexual acts	2,160	34.6
Inmate-on-inmate abusive sexual contacts	611	9.8
Staff sexual misconduct	2,386	38.2
Staff sexual harassment	1,084	17.4

Approximately 15% of allegations of nonconsensual sexual acts in 2005 were substantiated

Allegations reported in 2005 were classified as:

• *substantiated*, if they were determined to have occurred
• *unsubstantiated*, if the evidence was insufficient to make a final determination that they occurred
• *unfounded*, if they were determined not to have occurred
• *investigation ongoing*, if a final determination had not been made at time of data collection.

Overall, inmate-on-inmate allegations of nonconsensual sexual violence were less likely to be substantiated than allegations of staff sexual misconduct. Based on allegations in State and

Federal prisons for which investigations had been completed, 14% of nonconsensual sexual acts were substantiated, compared to 15% of allegations of staff sexual misconduct (table 3). In jails 16% of completed investigations of nonconsensual sexual acts were substantiated, compared to 37% of the allegations of staff sexual misconduct.

The most common outcome of investigations of sexual violence was a determination of lack of evidence. More than 66% of allegations of staff sexual misconduct in prison and 49% of allegations of inmate-on-inmate nonconsensual sexual acts were unsubstantiated. More than a third of completed investigations of nonconsensual sexual acts in State and Federal prisons (37%) and local jails (38%) were determined to be unfounded.

During 2005 correctional authorities substantiated 885 incidents of sexual violence

The survey of administrative records recorded 620 substantiated incidents of sexual violence. Taking into account sampling of local jails, private prisons or jails, and jails in Indian country, the estimated total for the Nation was 885. Relative to the number of inmates, there were 0.40 substantiated incidents of sexual violence per 1,000 inmates reported in 2005, down from the 0.55 per 1,000 inmates in adult facilities in 2004.

Number of substantiated incidents of sexual violence

Facility type	National estimate	Rate per 1,000 inmates
Total	885	0.40
Prisons		
Public - Federal	41	0.26
Public - State	458	0.39
Private	24	0.24
Local jails		
Public	336	0.45
Private	13	0.78
Other adult facilities		
Indian country jails*	10	^
Military-operated	2	0.77
ICE-operated	1	0.15

*Excludes facilities housing juveniles only.
^Too few cases to provide a reliable rate.

Table 3. Allegations of sexual violence in Federal and State prisons, local jails, and private prisons and jails, 2005

	State and Federal prisons		Local jails		Private prisons and jails	
	Number	Percent*	Number	Percent*	Number	Percent*
Inmate-on-inmate nonconsensual sexual acts	1,443	100.0%	263	100.0%	34	100.0%
Substantiated	163	13.7	32	15.8	7	31.8
Unsubstantiated	582	49.0	94	46.3	13	59.1
Unfounded	442	37.2	78	37.9	2	9.1
Investigation ongoing	236		32		12	
Inmate-on-inmate abusive sexual contacts	423	100.0%	57	100.0%	3	100.0%
Substantiated	103	25.8	12	22.6	0	0
Unsubstantiated	235	58.8	17	32.1	3	100.0
Unfounded	62	15.5	24	45.3	0	0
Investigation ongoing	13		4		0	
Staff sexual misconduct	1,829	100.0%	184	100.0%	29	100.0%
Substantiated	195	14.9	53	36.5	6	20.7
Unsubstantiated	867	66.4	50	34.5	18	62.1
Unfounded	243	18.6	42	29.0	5	17.2
Investigation ongoing	519		39		0	
Staff sexual harassment	914	100.0%	39	100.0%	7	100.0%
Substantiated	39	5.7	3	10.0	0	0
Unsubstantiated	478	69.4	12	40.0	7	100.0
Unfounded	172	25.0	15	50.0	0	0
Investigation ongoing	226		8		0	

Note: Excludes facilities operated by the U.S. military, the Bureau of Immigration and Customs Enforcement, tribal authorities and the Bureau of Indian Affairs.
*Percents based on allegations for which investigations had been completed.

Correctional authorities provided detail on 82% of substantiated incidents

For the first time in the 2005 survey prison systems and sampled facilities were asked to provide detailed information on each substantiated incident of sexual violence. Using a separate incident form, the survey obtained incident-based data, providing a basis for an in-depth analysis of sexual violence. Data included details on the circumstances surrounding each incident, characteristics of victims and perpetrators, type of pressure or physical force, sanctions imposed and victim assistance.

Incident-level data were reported on 510 of the 620 substantiated incidents (82%). More than two-thirds of the unreported incidents were in the Federal system (missing data on 35 incidents of inmate-on-inmate sexual violence), New Hampshire (missing 23 incident reports), and Vermont (missing 16 reports on staff sexual harassment). An additional 25 substantiated incidents were missing from local jail reports. Because most systems and facilities reported fully, there was little evidence of any selection bias among the 510 incident reports.

Data provided on substantiated incidents of inmate-on-inmate sexual violence revealed that —

• In 4% of the incidents more than one inmate was victimized (table 4).
• In 7% of the incidents there was more than one perpetrator (table 5).
• Males comprised 88% of the victims and 91% of the perpetrators in prison and jails.
• 74% of victims in jail and 42% in prison were age 24 or younger; while 42% of perpetrators in jail and 66% in prison were age 30 or older.

• Whites comprised 73% of the victims, 43% of the perpetrators; while blacks comprised 12% of victims, 39% of perpetrators.
• 15% of perpetrators were Hispanic, compared to 9% of victims.
• More than half of inmate-on-inmate sexual violence was interracial: 10% involved a white perpetrator and a non-white victim; 31% black perpetrators and a non-black victim; 11% a Hispanic perpetrator on a non-Hispanic victim (not shown).

Number of victims and perpetrators by race/Hispanic origin

Victim	Perpetrator			
	White*	Black*	Hispanic	Other*
Total	171	152	65	13
White*	130	113	39	10
Black*	15	28	4	0
Hispanic	6	11	21	1
Other*	20	0	1	2

*Excludes persons of Hispanic origin.

Table 4. Characteristics of victims in substantiated incidents of inmate-on-inmate sexual violence, by type, 2005

	All facilities[a]	Prison	Jail
Number of incidents	358	208	127
Number of victims			
1	95.8%	94.7%	96.9%
2	3.1	3.4	3.1
3	0.3	0.5	0
4 or more	0.8	1.4	0
Gender[b]			
Male	88.4%	84.8%	92.4%
Female	11.6	15.2	7.6
Age[b]			
Under 18	7.7%	0.9%	20.6%
18-24	45.1	41.4	53.4
25-29	12.5	15.8	3.8
30-34	17.0	18.1	10.7
35-39	9.3	11.2	7.6
40-44	4.8	6.5	3.1
45 or older	3.7	6.0	0.8
Race/Hispanic origin[b]			
White[c]	72.7%	78.1%	71.0%
Black[c]	11.9	10.2	11.5
Hispanic	9.3	9.8	3.8
Other[c,d]	6.1	1.9	13.7

[a]Includes substantiated incidents reported by private prisons and jails, Indian country jails, and facilities operated by the U.S. military and ICE.

[b]Based on characteristics of victims for whom gender (380), age (377), or race/Hispanic origin (377) were reported.

[c]Excludes victims of Hispanic origin.

[d]Includes American Indians, Alaska Natives, Asians, Native Hawaiians, and Other Pacific Islanders.

Table 5. Characteristics of perpetrators in substantiated incidents of inmate-on-inmate sexual violence, by type, 2005

	All facilities[a]	Prison	Jail
Number of perpetrators			
1	92.7%	92.8%	91.4%
2	3.6	3.9	3.9
3	1.4	1.9	0.8
4 or more	2.3	1.5	3.9
Gender[b]			
Male	91.3%	85.7%	98.6%
Female	8.7	14.3	1.4
Age[b]			
Under 18	5.4%	0.5%	14.7%
18-24	20.1	16.8	30.1
25-29	14.9	16.8	13.2
30-34	14.9	15.0	9.6
35-39	14.7	17.3	6.6
40-44	18.0	16.4	19.9
45 or older	11.9	17.3	5.9
Race/Hispanic origin[b]			
White[c]	43.0%	42.1%	48.2%
Black[c]	38.8	42.1	33.6
Hispanic	14.7	10.0	18.2
Other[c,d]	3.4	5.9	0

[a]Includes substantiated incidents reported by private prisons and jails, Indian country jails, and facilities operated by the U.S. military and ICE.

[b]Based on characteristics of perpetrators for whom gender (401), age (388), or race/Hispanic origin (381) were reported.

[c]Excludes perpetrators of Hispanic origin.

[d]Includes American Indians, Alaska Natives, Asians, Native Hawaiians, and Other Pacific Islanders.

Physical force or threat of force was used in 51% of inmate-on-inmate sexual violence

Correctional authorities reported that force or threat of force was involved in about half of all incidents of inmate-on-inmate sexual violence (table 6). In less than a third of the incidents no force was used or threatened. In other incidents of inmate sexual violence, victims were talked into it (18%), bribed/blackmailed (11%), or offered protection from other inmates (6%).

Force was more common among incidents of nonconsensual sexual activity than among incidents of abusive sexual contacts. In nearly a third of nonconsensual sexual acts, the victim was physically held down or restrained. In a sixth, the victim was physically harmed or injured.

In more than two-thirds of the inmate-on-inmate incidents, the sexual violence occurred in the victim's cell (59%) or in a dormitory (12%). In only 21% of the substantiated incidents did the sexual violence occur in a common area, such as a shower or a day room. In less than 9% of the incidents, the inmate-on-inmate sexual violence occurred in a program service area, such as in a storage room, hallway, laundry, cafeteria, kitchen or workshop.

Incidents of inmate sexual violence were the most common (44%) in the evening between 6 p.m. and midnight and the least common (18%) overnight between midnight and 6 a.m. The most serious forms of inmate sexual violence (nonconsensual sexual acts) were most likely to have occurred in the evening (50%); while the least serious acts (abusive sexual contacts) were most likely to have occurred in the morning between 6 a.m. and noon (41%).

In nearly 90% of the substantiated incidents of inmate sexual violence, the victim or another inmate reported the incident. In less than 11% of the incidents had a correctional officer made the initial report. In only 4% of the most serious incidents (nonconsensual sexual acts) had medical or health care staff reported the incident.

Table 6. Circumstances surrounding substantiated incidents of inmate-on-inmate sexual violence, by type, 2005

	All facilities*	Prison	Jail	Noncon-sensual sexual acts	Abusive sexual contacts
Number of incidents	357	207	127	241	116
Type of pressure or force					
None	30.5%	25.1%	40.2%	17.8%	56.9%
Force/threat of force	50.7	61.4	39.4	58.9	32.8
Threatened with physical harm	22.4	32.4	10.2	26.1	15.5
Physically held down or restrained	28.3	32.9	23.6	32.4	19.0
Physically harmed or injured	12.6	13.0	13.4	16.5	5.2
Threatened with a weapon	4.2	6.8	0.8	5.8	0.9
Persuasion or talked into it	18.5	15.9	15.7	22.4	10.3
Bribery/blackmail	10.9	7.7	11.8	12.9	6.9
Gave victim drugs/alcohol	0.3	0.5	0	0.4	0
Offered protection from other inmates	5.9	6.8	5.5	8.3	0.9
Where occurred					
In victim's cell/room	59.1%	58.7%	60.2%	59.2%	58.6%
In perpetrator's cell/room	3.9	5.3	0	5.0	1.7
In a dormitory	12.1	7.8	17.3	10.8	15.4
In a common area	20.7	18.0	25.8	23.3	15.5
In temporary holding area	0.3	0	0.8	0	0.9
In a program service area	8.7	12.6	3.1	2.9	20.7
Outside the facility	1.1	1.9	0	1.3	0.9
While in transit	0.3	0.5	0	0.4	0
Time of day					
6 a.m. to noon	27.8%	22.0%	36.0%	21.5%	41.3%
Noon to 6 p.m.	20.5	30.9	4.8	18.4	24.8
6 p.m. to midnight	44.0	44.5	42.4	50.2	31.2
Midnight to 6 a.m.	18.4	18.8	20.0	18.5	18.2
Who reported the incident					
Victim	82.6%	80.2%	90.6%	84.2%	78.6%
Another inmate	8.4	9.7	7.1	7.9	10.3
Family of victim	0.6	0.5	0.8	0.4	0.9
Correctional officer	10.6	12.1	6.3	10.8	10.3
Administrative staff	0.6	0	1.6	0.8	0
Medical/healthcare staff	2.8	2.4	1.6	4.1	0
Counselor/teacher	1.4	2.4	0	0.4	3.4
Chaplain/other religious official	0.3	0.5	0	0.4	0

Note: Detail may sum to more than 100% because multiple responses were allowed for each item.
*Includes substantiated incidents reported by private prisons and jails, Indian country jails, and facilities operated by the U.S. military and ICE.

Victims received physical injuries in 15% of substantiated incidents of inmate-on-inmate sexual violence

In most substantiated incidents of inmate-on-inmate sexual violence victims were not physically injured (85%) (table 7). Anal or rectal tearing was reported in 6% of the incidents; less serious injuries, including bruises, black eyes, sprains, cuts, and scratches were reported in 11% of the incidents. In fewer than 1% of the incidents, victims received broken bones or were knocked unconscious.

Knife or stab wounds and other internal injuries were not reported for any of the incidents.

Victims received medical attention, counseling or mental health treatment in more than two-thirds of the incidents of nonconsensual sexual acts. Among the most serious incidents, 63% of the victims were given a medical examination; 27% were administered a rape kit; 17% were tested for HIV/AIDS; 17% were tested for other sexually transmitted diseases; and 33% were provided counseling or mental health treatment.

Half of victims of nonconsensual sexual acts were placed in protective custody or administrative segregation

The most common response following a reported incident of sexual violence was to place the victim in administrative segregation or protective custody (44%) or to transfer the victim to another facility (11%). Given differing housing options, prison authorities were more likely than jail authorities to move the victims rather than confine them to their cell/room.

Victims of abusive sexual contacts were the least likely to be moved, with over half (53%) having no change in housing. About a third of the victims of nonconsensual sexual acts were confined to their cell (11%) or had no change in their housing (23%).

Most inmate perpetrators received legal sanctions or solitary confinement

• A legal sanction, including arrest, referral for prosecution, or new sentence, was imposed on perpetrators in 31% of the substantiated incidents in prisons; 83% of the incidents in jails.
• Perpetrators were referred for prosecution in more than half of the substantiated incidents of nonconsensual sexual acts; in a third of the incidents of abusive sexual contacts.
• Perpetrators were moved to solitary confinement in 72% of the incidents of nonconsensual sexual acts and in 70% of the incidents of abusive sexual contacts.
• Perpetrators also received other sanctions, including confinement to own cell/room (28%), loss of privileges (21%), placement in a higher custody level (20%), or transfer to another facility (19%).

Table 7. Impact on victims and perpetrators in substantiated incidents of inmate-on-inmate sexual violence, by type, 2005

	All facilities[a]	Prison	Jail	Noncon-sensual sexual acts	Abusive sexual contacts
Victim injured					
No	84.6%	80.0%	95.7%	78.4%	96.6%
Yes[b]	15.4	20.0	4.3	21.6	3.4
Broken bones	0.3	0.5	0	0.4	0
Anal/vaginal tearing	6.1	5.4	2.6	9.3	0
Teeth chipped/knocked out	0.3	0	0.9	0	0.9
Knocked unconscious	0.3	0.5	0	0.4	0
Bruises, black eye, sprains, cuts, scratches, swelling	11.0	15.6	2.6	15.0	3.4
Medical follow up for victim					
Given medical examination	53.4%	58.9%	42.5%	63.3%	33.3%
Administered rape kit	19.0	21.3	8.7	26.7	3.4
Tested for HIV/AIDS	12.0	14.0	6.3	17.0	1.7
Tested for other STD	11.8	14.0	5.5	16.6	1.7
Provided counseling or mental health treatment	34.9	43.5	20.3	32.9	39.3
None of the above	35.7	29.0	46.9	31.7	43.6
Change in housing/custody for victim[c]					
Placed in administrative segregation or protective custody	44.0%	46.6%	40.2%	49.3%	30.3%
Placed in medical unit	8.7	13.2	2.0	9.1	7.8
Confined to own cell/room	9.0	3.2	18.6	10.5	5.6
Transferred to another facility	10.7	17.5	0.0	12.3	6.7
Other (reported after release/transfer)	4.8	2.6	1.0	6.0	2.2
None of the above	31.7	30.7	38.2	23.2	52.8
Sanction imposed on perpetrator					
Solitary/disciplinary	70.8%	84.5%	55.9%	71.6%	69.6%
Confined to own cell/room	27.9	21.8	40.2	25.1	33.0
Placed in higher custody	20.1	16.6	26.8	27.3	5.4
Transferred to another facility	18.9	25.4	9.4	17.7	21.2
Loss of good time	13.4	22.8	0	13.9	12.5
Given extra work	0.6	0.5	0	0.4	0.9
Loss of privileges	20.7	21.2	22.0	21.6	18.8
Legal action	51.3	31.1	83.5	57.6	39.3
Arrested	12.2	4.1	20.5	15.9	4.5
Referred for prosecution	45.6	28.5	77.3	50.6	34.8
Given new sentence	4.1	1.0	9.4	6.1	0
Disciplinary report issued	4.7	8.3	0	6.1	1.8

Note: Detail may sum to more than 100% because multiple responses were allowed for each item.

[a]Includes substantiated incidents reported by private prisons and jails, Indian country jails, and facilities operated by the U.S. military and ICE.

[b]The categories "knife or stab wounds" and "internal injuries" were not marked in any incident.

[c]The category "given a higher custody level within the facility" was not marked in any incident.

Two-thirds of incidents of staff sexual misconduct with inmates were reported to be romantic

The survey collected data on 344 substantiated incidents of staff sexual misconduct and harassment during 2005. In two-thirds of these incidents, correctional authorities determined that staff had a romantic relationship with the inmate (table 8). Although legally all sexual relationships between staff and inmates are considered nonconsensual, fewer than 15% of the substantiated incidents involved physical force, abuse of power or pressure by staff.

Coercion, including force, pressure, unwanted touching, indecent exposure, and harassment, was more common among incidents in jails (43%) than in prisons (26%).

Other data reported on substantiated incidents of staff sexual misconduct and harassment revealed that —

• In more than half the incidents, either the victim (32%) or another inmate (26%) reported the misconduct (table 9).
• In a third of the incidents, correctional officers (18%) or administrative staff (16%) reported the incident. In 10% of the incidents, the misconduct was reported anonymously.
• Most incidents of staff sexual misconduct and harassment occurred outside of the inmate's living area, in a program area (53%), outside of the facility (12%), or in a common area (10%).
• In prisons, incidents of staff sexual misconduct occurred most often between noon and 6 p.m. (50%); in jails, incidents occurred more evenly throughout the day.
• In 5% of the incidents more than one staff member was involved in the sexual misconduct.
• In 10% of the incidents more than one inmate was involved.

Female staff implicated in staff sexual misconduct in prisons; males in local jails

Characteristics of victims and perpetrators of staff sexual misconduct and harassment differed among prisons and jail facilities:

• In State and Federal prisons 67% of the victims of staff misconduct were male, while 62% of the perpetrators were female (tables 10 and 11).
• In local jails 78% of the victims were females; 87% of the perpetrators, male.
• 47% of the prison staff involved in sexual misconduct and harassment were age 40 or older; compared to 27% of the jail staff.
• In prisons 69% of the perpetrators were white, 25% black, and 3% Hispanic.
• In jails 74% of the perpetrators were white, 21% black, and 4% Hispanic.

Table 8. Characteristics of substantiated incidents of staff sexual misconduct and harassment, by type of facility, 2005

Characteristic	All facilities*	Prison	Jail
Number of incidents	344	208	111
Nature of the incident			
Romantic	68.3%	73.6%	56.8%
Sexual harassment	10.9	12.0	10.9
Unwanted touching	10.3	9.6	10.8
Indecent exposure	5.3	4.8	7.2
Pressure/abuse of power	14.1	10.6	21.6
Physical force	0.6	1.0	0
Number of staff involved			
1	95.0%	95.7%	92.8%
2	5.0	4.3	7.2
Number of victims			
1	90.1%	92.8%	84.7%
2	8.1	4.8	14.4
3	0.6	1.0	0
4 or more	1.2	1.5	0.9

Note: Detail may sum to more than 100% because multiple responses were allowed for each item.
*Includes substantiated incidents reported by private prisons and jails, Indian country jails, and facilities operated by the U.S. military and ICE.

Table 9. Circumstances surrounding substantiated incidents of staff sexual misconduct and harassment, by type of facility, 2005

Characteristic	All facilities[a]	Prison	Jail
Who reported the incident			
Victim	31.9%	24.9%	43.9%
Another inmate	25.8	28.9	26.2
Family of victim	0.9	0.5	1.9
Correctional officer	17.6	18.8	11.2
Administrative staff	15.8	16.2	18.7
Medical/healthcare staff	2.4	2.5	0
Instructor/teacher/counselor	0.9	1.5	0
Chaplain/other religious official	0.3	0.5	0
Other (anonymous/letter)	9.7	11.7	4.7
Where occurred[b]			
In victim's cell/room	14.0%	8.9%	26.1%
In a dormitory	6.7	8.9	3.6
In a common area	10.1	7.3	17.3
In temporary holding area	0.6	0.5	0.9
In a program service area	52.6	57.3	40.5
Outside the facility	12.5	13.0	12.7
Other/unknown	9.7	12.5	2.7
Time of day			
6 a.m. to noon	32.4%	37.0%	30.5%
Noon to 6 p.m.	41.4	50.0	29.5
6 p.m. to midnight	36.8	36.4	32.4
Midnight to 6 a.m.	18.5	16.9	23.6

Note: Detail may sum to more than 100% because multiple responses were allowed for each item.
[a]Includes substantiated incidents reported by private prisons and jails, Indian country jails, and facilities operated by the U.S. military and ICE.
[b]The category "In transit" was not marked in any incident.

Table 10. Characteristics of staff involved in staff sexual misconduct and harassment, by type of facility, 2005

	All facilities[a]	Prison	Jail
Gender[b]			
Male	54.3%	37.7%	86.6%
Female	45.7	62.3	13.4
Age[b]			
24 or younger	12.7%	10.4%	10.5%
25-29	14.7	13.3	14.9
30-34	15.9	13.7	21.9
35-39	19.0	15.2	25.4
40-44	14.1	13.7	17.5
45-54	18.2	25.1	8.8
55 or older	5.5	8.5	0.9
Race/Hispanic origin[b]			
White[c]	68.5%	69.4%	74.4%
Black[c]	23.5	25.4	21.4
Hispanic	4.3	2.9	4.3
Other[c,d]	3.7	2.4	0

Note: Detail may sum to more than 100% because multiple responses were allowed for each item.

[a]Includes substantiated incidents reported by private prisons and jails, Indian country jails, and facilities operated by the U.S. military and ICE.

[b]The number of staff involved totaled 358. Gender was reported for 350 staff; age for 347; and race/Hispanic origin for 349.

[c]Excludes staff of Hispanic origin.

[d]Includes American Indians, Alaska Natives, Asians, Native Hawaiians, and Other Pacific Islanders.

Table 11. Characteristics of inmates involved in staff sexual misconduct and harassment, by type of facility, 2005

	All facilities[a]	Prison	Jail
Gender[b]			
Male	52.0%	67.5%	21.9%
Female	48.0	32.5	78.1
Age [b]			
Under 18	0.6%	0%	1.7%
18-24	17.6	12.8	24.4
25-29	28.5	25.1	26.9
30-34	22.9	27.5	18.5
35-39	17.3	18.0	18.5
40-44	6.7	8.5	5.0
45 or older	6.4	8.1	5.0
Race/Hispanic origin[b]			
White[c]	56.8%	54.2%	66.7%
Black[c]	26.9	32.1	24.0
Hispanic	9.8	9.4	6.2
Other[c,d]	6.5	4.2	3.1

[a]Includes substantiated incidents reported by private prisons and jails, Indian country jails, and facilities operated by the U.S. military and ICE.

[b]The number of victims of staff misconduct totaled 390: gender was reported for 367; age for 358; and race/Hispanic origin for 368.

[c]Excludes inmates of Hispanic origin.

[d]Includes American Indians, Alaska Natives, Asians, Native Hawaiians, and Other Pacific Islanders.

Among victims of staff sexual misconduct, white inmates were over-represented, compared with the general inmate population. Non-Hispanic whites comprised 57% of the inmates involved in staff misconduct, compared to 36% of all prison and jail inmates at midyear 2005. (See *Prison and Jail Inmates at Midyear 2005*, NCJ 213133.) Non-Hispanic blacks comprised 27% of inmates involved in staff misconduct; 40% of all inmates nationwide. Hispanic inmates were 10% of the victims of staff misconduct compared to 20% of the inmate population.

Over two-thirds of perpetrators of staff sexual misconduct or harassment were correctional officers

Most substantiated incidents of staff sexual misconduct and harassment involved correctional officers — 57% of the incidents in prisons; 89% of those in jails (table 12). In prisons, nearly 16% of perpetrators of staff misconduct were maintenance and other facility support staff, including groundskeepers, janitors, cooks, and drivers. An additional 10% of perpetrators in prisons were medical or health care staff, including counselors, doctors, dentists, nurses, psychologists, psychiatrists, social workers, and medical assistants.

In both prisons and jails, about 13% of the staff perpetrators of sexual misconduct or harassment were contract employees or vendors.

Inmates involved in staff sexual misconduct often transferred or placed in segregation

In 27% of the substantiated incidents of staff sexual misconduct the inmates involved were transferred to another facility; in 20% of the incidents they were placed in administrative segregation or protective custody (table 13). In incidents involving a romantic relationship between inmate and staff, more than half of the inmates were either transferred (30%) or placed in administrative segregation (22%) (not shown).

In incidents involving staff coercion, about a third of the victims were either transferred (20%) or placed in segregation (15%).

In most substantiated incidents of staff sexual misconduct (74%), victims received no medical followup, counseling, or mental health treatment. Excluding incidents involving romantic relationships, victims in 15% of the nonconsensual acts were given a medical examination and 19% were provided counseling or mental health treatment.

Table 12. Type of staff involved in staff sexual misconduct and harassment, by type of facility, 2005

	All facilities*	Prison	Jail
Type of staff involved			
Full/part-time employee	86.7%	86.2%	87.9%
Contract employee/vendor	13.3	13.8	12.1
Volunteer/intern	0.6	1.0	0
Position of staff involved			
Administrator	1.8%	2.9%	0%
Correctional officer	68.7	57.0	89.1
Clerical	3.5	3.9	3.6
Maintenance	10.9	15.9	0.9
Medical/health care	6.2	9.7	0.9
Educational	2.6	3.9	0.9
Other program staff	1.5	2.4	0
Other	6.8	5.3	9.1

*Includes substantiated incidents reported by private prisons and jails, Indian country jails, and facilities operated by the U.S. military and ICE.

Nearly 90% of perpetrators of staff misconduct arrested, referred for prosecution, or discharged

Correctional authorities indicated that in 82% of the substantiated incidents staff had been discharged or resigned; 45% arrested or referred for prosecution, and 17% were disciplined, transferred, or demoted.

Among the multiple types of sanctions imposed on staff, discharge or resignation was the most common — 30% of the incidents in prison and 55% of those in jails. Many staff chose to resign (43%) rather than be terminated. In incidents involving a romantic relationship between an inmate and staff, 90% of staff were discharged or resigned (not shown). In incidents involving coercion, 64% of staff lost their jobs and 53% were arrested or referred for prosecution.

Methodology

The 2005 Survey of Sexual Violence was based on seven separate samples, corresponding to the different facilities covered under the act. The following samples were drawn:

1. The survey included all 50 State adult prison systems and the Federal Bureau of Prisons. Prison administrators were directed to report only on incidents of sexual violence that occurred within publicly operated adult facilities.

2. A sample of 32 privately operated prison facilities was drawn to represent a 10% sample of the 319 private prisons identified in the 2000 Census of State and Federal Adult Correctional Facilities and updated for new construction and closures since 2000. Facilities were sorted by region and average daily population and then sampled with probabilities proportionate to size. One sampled facility had closed.

3. Publicly operated jail facilities were selected based on data reported in the 2004 Deaths in Custody collection.

Jurisdictions were sorted into 6 strata, based on their average daily popula-

tions, and then sampled systematically, to provide a representative national sample. A total of 72 jurisdictions were sampled with certainty (corresponding to the largest jurisdiction in each State plus 26 jurisdictions selected due to their large size). An additional 278 jurisdictions were selected from 4 strata, with probabilities of selection proportionate to size. Jail administrators were directed to report on all publicly operated facilities within their jurisdiction. Of the 350 selected facilities, 3 had closed.

4. A sample of 5 privately operated jails was also selected based on the data reported in the 2004 Deaths in Custody collection. The 38 private facilities were sorted by region and their average daily population during 2004. Facilities were selected systematically using a random start and a fixed sampling interval.

5. Three additional samples of other correctional facilities were drawn to represent:

a) jails in Indian country (7 facilities holding adults were selected from a total of 68 based on probabilities proportionate to size);

b) military-operated facilities (all of the 59 facilities operated by the Armed Services in the continental U.S.);

c) 14 facilities operated by the Bureau of Immigration and Customs Enforcement.

Data for each correctional system and sampled facility are displayed in the *Appendix tables*. In each table a measure of population size has been provided as a basis of comparison; however, the survey results should not be used to rank systems or facilities. Variations in the number of allegations and substantiated incidents may reflect differences in definitions and reporting criteria, as well as variations in procedures for recording allegations and in the thoroughness of subsequent investigations.

Table 13. Impact on inmate and staff in substantiated incidents of staff sexual misconduct and harassment, 2005

	All facilities[a]	Prison	Jail
Medical followup for inmate			
Given medical examination	14.7%	11.6%	17.1%
Administered rape kit	7.4	2.6	11.8
Tested for HIV/AIDS	1.5	0.5	1.8
Tested for other STD	2.5	1.6	2.7
Provided counseling or mental health treatment	14.2	17.4	10.9
None of the above	74.2	78.4	67.6
Any change in housing/custody for inmate			
Placed in administratve segregation or protective custody	19.7%	26.3%	3.0%
Placed in medical unit	2.2	0	4.0
Confined to own cell/room	5.1	1.1	11.1
Given a higher custody level within facility	4.5	4.7	1.0
Transferred to another facility	26.8	25.3	35.4
Other[b]	11.1	7.4	17.2
None of the above	36.3	42.6	28.3
Sanctions on staff			
Legal sanction	44.7%	37.0%	62.7%
Arrested	27.9	16.8	48.6
Referred for prosecution	34.3	34.6	35.1
Loss of job	81.8	81.7	79.3
Discharged	41.3	30.3	55.5
Staff resigned (prior to investigation)	30.1	32.7	27.0
Staff resigned (after investigation)	13.2	19.7	3.6
Other sanction	17.0	16.8	19.8
Reprimanded/disciplined	11.8	12.5	11.8
Demoted/diminished responsibilities	3.5	1.0	8.1
Transferred to another facility	2.3	3.4	0

Note: Detail may sum to more than 100% because multiple responses were allowed for each item.

[a]Includes substantiated incidents reported by private prisons and jails, Indian country jails, and facilities operated by the U.S. military and ICE.

[b]Includes "stayed in same unit," "transferred elsewhere in facility," and "incident reported after release."

NCJ 214646

The Bureau of Justice Statistics is the statistical agency of the U.S. Department of Justice. Jeffrey L. Sedgwick is director.

Allen J. Beck and Paige M. Harrison wrote this report. Laura Maruschak, Seri Palla, and Maura Spiegelman verified the report. Tina Dorsey, Carolyn Williams, and Marianne W. Zawitz produced and edited the report. Jayne Robinson prepared the report for publication.

Timothy A. Hughes and Paige M. Harrison, under the supervision of Allen J. Beck, designed the survey, developed the questionnaires, and monitored data collection and data processing.

Pamela H. Butler, Greta B. Clark, and Nicole D. Simpson carried out data collection and processing, under the supervision of Charlene M. Sebold, Governments Division, Census Bureau, U.S. Department of Commerce. Patricia D. Torreyson, Pearl E. Chase, and D. Alicia Gumbs assisted in data collection. Suzanne M. Dorinski drew the facility samples and provided sampling weights.

July 2006, NCJ 214646

This report in portable document format and in ASCII and its related statistical data and tables—including five appendix tables—are available at the BJS World Wide Web Internet site: <http://www.ojp.usdoj.gov/bjs/>

Office of Justice Programs

Partnerships for Safer Communities
http://www.ojp.usdoj.gov

Appendix table 1a. Allegations of inmate-on-inmate sexual violence reported by State or Federal prison authorities, by type, 2005

Jurisdiction	Prisoners in custody, 6/30/2005[a]	Reported inmate-on-inmate nonconsensual sexual acts					Reported inmate-on-inmate abusive sexual contacts				
		Allega-tions	Sub-stantiated	Unsub-stantiated	Unfounded	Investi-gation ongoing	Allega-tions	Sub-stantiated	Unsub-stantiated	Unfounded	Investi-gation ongoing
Total	1,337,473	1,443	163	582	442	236	423	103	235	62	13
Federal[b]	156,643	25	5	/	/	/	40	30	/	/	/
State	1,180,830	1,418	158	582	442	236	383	73	235	62	13
Alabama	25,161	9	1	4	4	0	1	0	0	1	0
Alaska	3,248	1	1	0	0	0	/	/	/	/	/
Arizona	27,204	17	6	4	6	1	6	2	1	3	0
Arkansas	12,568	7	1	3	1	2	0	0	0	0	0
California	161,709	59	4	28	16	11	16	2	8	0	6
Colorado	16,997	27	15	8	4	0	11	8	3	0	0
Connecticut[c]	19,087	21	0	20	1	0	/	/	/	/	/
Delaware	6,916	2	0	0	2	0	1	0	0	1	0
Florida	79,478	124	0	101	14	9	19	0	14	5	0
Georgia[c]	43,057	37	0	0	4	33	/	/	/	/	/
Hawaii[c]	3,931	8	4	3	1	0	/	/	/	/	/
Idaho	6,136	15	3	5	7	0	11	5	6	0	0
Illinois	44,669	17	1	14	0	2	0	0	0	0	0
Indiana	22,304	27	3	12	11	1	3	0	1	2	0
Iowa	8,578	11	0	5	3	3	8	0	0	8	0
Kansas	9,068	25	1	7	16	1	17	1	14	1	1
Kentucky	11,366	3	0	2	1	0	10	4	4	2	0
Louisiana	16,667	10	1	6	1	2	1	0	0	1	0
Maine	2,063	4	3	0	1	0	0	0	0	0	0
Maryland	23,086	15	2	10	0	3	1	1	0	0	0
Massachusetts	10,159	10	2	2	5	1	21	9	2	10	0
Michigan[c]	48,535	48	19	29	0	0	/	/	/	/	/
Minnesota	7,996	12	1	2	9	0	1	1	0	0	0
Mississippi	11,643	1	0	1	0	0	0	0	0	0	0
Missouri	31,000	36	1	25	5	5	21	4	11	2	4
Montana	1,911	2	2	0	0	0	3	2	1	0	0
Nebraska[c]	4,308	10	0	0	10	0	/	/	/	/	/
Nevada[c]	11,155	14	0	7	2	5	/	/	/	/	/
New Hampshire[c,d,e]	2,456	18	18	/	/	/	/	/	/	/	/
New Jersey[c]	26,353	3	0	0	2	1	/	/	/	/	/
New Mexico	3,757	0	0	0	0	0	0	0	0	0	0
New York	63,234	28	1	14	0	13	1	1	0	0	0
North Carolina[c]	36,477	20	7	12	1	0	/	/	/	/	/
North Dakota	1,287	1	0	0	1	0	8	4	1	3	0
Ohio	42,346	71	11	10	50	0	27	12	6	9	0
Oklahoma[a]	17,196	23	3	10	10	0	2	1	1	0	0
Oregon	12,769	25	4	15	2	4	3	0	3	0	0
Pennsylvania[c]	40,649	16	6	10	0	0	/	/	/	/	/
Rhode Island	3,364	1	1	0	0	0	3	1	1	1	0
South Carolina[d]	23,057	0	0	0	0	0	0	0	0	0	0
South Dakota	3,385	6	1	3	2	0	7	2	3	2	0
Tennessee	14,303	25	3	12	7	3	7	2	2	1	2
Texas	141,247	511	10	145	225	131	143	5	131	7	0
Utah	4,775	14	3	8	3	0	7	3	2	2	0
Vermont[e]	1,601	19	1	17	1	0	20	1	18	1	0
Virginia[e]	29,445	7	1	0	4	2	0	0	0	0	0
Washington	16,126	25	7	12	5	1	0	0	0	0	0
West Virginia	3,966	3	2	0	0	1	1	1	0	0	0
Wisconsin[f]	21,850	24	6	13	4	1	/	/	/	/	/
Wyoming	1,187	6	2	3	1	0	3	1	2	0	0

/Not reported.

[a]Excludes inmates in private facilities. Counts were based on National Prisoners Statistics (NPS-1A), 2005.

[b]Allegations were reported for occurrences in 2005; findings may include cases from previous years.

[c] Allegations of abusive sexual contacts could not be counted separately from allegations of nonconsensual sexual acts.

[d]Allegations limited to substantiated occurrences only.

[e]Allegations limited to completed acts only.

[f]Reports of abusive sexual contacts were based on a broader category of inmate sexual misconduct.

Jurisdiction	Reported allegations of staff sexual misconduct with inmates					Reported allegations of staff sexual harassment of inmates				
	Allega-tions	Sub-stantiated	Unsub-stantiated	Unfounded	Investi-gation ongoing	Allega-tions	Sub-stantiated	Unsub-stantiated	Unfounded	Investi-gation ongoing
Total	1,829	195	867	243	519	914	39	478	172	226
Federal[a,b]	203	6	80	5	107	/	/	/	/	/
State	1,626	189	787	238	412	914	39	478	172	226
Alabama	2	0	0	2	0	1	0	0	1	0
Alaska	1	1	0	0	0	0	0	0	0	0
Arizona	63	3	35	24	1	1	0	0	1	0
Arkansas	29	5	4	15	5	2	0	1	1	0
California	51	6	22	4	19	37	2	22	9	4
Colorado	21	9	2	4	6	8	0	1	5	2
Connecticut[a]	19	0	15	0	4	/	/	/	/	/
Delaware	2	0	0	2	0	1	1	0	0	0
Florida	264	5	232	15	12	77	0	67	1	9
Georgia	226	0	87	0	139	218	0	114	0	104
Hawaii	8	3	1	1	3	1	0	0	0	1
Idaho	10	3	2	3	2	4	0	0	4	0
Illinois	0	0	0	0	0	0	0	0	0	0
Indiana	35	15	9	10	1	13	2	8	3	0
Iowa	19	4	7	6	2	1	1	0	0	0
Kansas	48	5	25	8	10	12	0	12	0	0
Kentucky	13	5	5	3	0	0	0	0	0	0
Louisiana	73	8	44	7	14	48	0	33	8	7
Maine	2	1	0	1	0	7	3	2	1	1
Maryland	17	0	12	1	4	0	0	0	0	0
Massachusetts	70	4	12	21	33	6	0	2	1	3
Michigan	35	3	7	19	6	245	1	118	126	0
Minnesota	19	2	8	6	3	0	0	0	0	0
Mississippi	6	5	0	0	1	0	0	0	0	0
Missouri	54	2	41	4	7	42	3	31	0	9
Montana	0	0	0	0	0	0	0	0	0	0
Nebraska[a]	2	1	0	1	0	/	/	/	/	/
Nevada[a]	1	0	0	1	0	/	/	/	/	/
New Hampshire	6	4	2	0	0	5	1	2	2	0
New Jersey	9	2	5	1	1	3	1	2	0	0
New Mexico	0	0	0	0	0	0	0	0	0	0
New York	138	13	60	0	65	20	2	8	0	10
North Carolina[a,c]	14	13	0	1	0	/	/	/	/	/
North Dakota	4	1	0	3	0	0	0	0	0	0
Ohio	18	2	14	1	1	22	0	17	0	5
Oklahoma[a]	19	5	11	3	0	/	/	/	/	/
Oregon	35	13	0	14	8	3	0	0	3	0
Pennsylvania	39	7	24	0	8	8	0	5	0	3
Rhode Island	12	3	6	3	0	0	0	0	0	0
South Carolina[c]	1	1	0	0	0	0	0	0	0	0
South Dakota	4	1	1	2	0	0	0	0	0	0
Tennessee	20	8	7	2	3	4	1	1	0	2
Texas[a]	54	4	22	1	27	/	/	/	/	/
Utah	5	0	2	3	0	2	1	1	0	0
Vermont	15	4	4	7	0	115	16	29	6	64
Virginia	24	5	4	8	7	1	0	0	0	1
Washington	38	5	18	4	11	2	1	1	0	0
West Virginia	1	0	1	0	0	0	0	0	0	0
Wisconsin	77	7	35	27	8	4	2	1	0	1
Wyoming	3	1	1	0	1	1	1	0	0	0

/Not reported.

[a]Reports of staff sexual misconduct may include reports of staff sexual harassment.

[b]Excludes 5 cases disposed of administratively.

[c]Reports of staff sexual misconduct are based on substantiated allegations only.

[d]Reports of staff sexual harassment are not recorded in a central database.

Appendix table 2a. Allegations of inmate-on-inmate sexual violence reported by local jail authorities, by type, 2005

Jurisdiction and facility	Average daily population, 2005	Reported inmate-on-inmate nonconsensual sexual acts				Reported inmate-on-inmate abusive sexual contacts			
		Allega-tions	Sub-stantiated	Unsub-stantiated	Unfounded	Allega-tions	Sub-stantiated	Unsub-stantiated	Unfounded
Total	328,655	263	32	94	78	57	12	17	24
Alabama									
Attalla City	16	0	0	0	0	0	0	0	0
Autauga County	160	0	0	0	0	0	0	0	0
Bibb County	71	0	0	0	0	0	0	0	0
Chilton County	207	0	0	0	0	0	0	0	0
Crenshaw County[a]	44	0	0	0	0	/	/	/	/
Franklin County	94	0	0	0	0	0	0	0	0
Lipscomb City	6	0	0	0	0	0	0	0	0
Madison County	835	0	0	0	0	0	0	0	0
Mobile County[b]	1,433	1	0	1	0	0	0	0	0
Pickens County	83	0	0	0	0	0	0	0	0
Pleasant Grove City	2	0	0	0	0	0	0	0	0
Russell County	297	0	0	0	0	0	0	0	0
Alaska									
Unalaska City[a,b]	4	0	0	0	0	0	0	0	0
Arizona									
Maricopa County	9,515	9	0	6	3	2	0	2	0
Mohave County	441	0	0	0	0	0	0	0	0
Pinal County[a]	698	0	0	0	0	/	/	/	/
Arkansas									
Brinkley City[a]	7	0	0	0	0	/	/	/	/
Craighead County[a]	227	0	0	0	0	/	/	/	/
Dallas County[c]	66	0	0	0	0	/	/	/	/
Drew County[a]	40	0	0	0	0	/	/	/	/
Pulaski County Regional[b]	857	0	0	0	0	0	0	0	0
Warren City	2	0	0	0	0	0	0	0	0
California									
Calaveras County	76	0	0	0	0	0	0	0	0
Contra Costa County[a]	1,627	0	0	0	0	/	/	/	/
Fresno County	3,029	2	0	0	2	2	0	0	2
Kern County	2,198	1	0	1	0	2	1	1	0
Kings County	307	0	0	0	0	0	0	0	0
Los Angeles County	19,488	4	0	4	0	4	0	4	0
Nevada County	215	0	0	0	0	0	0	0	0
Orange County	6,164	2	0	2	0	1	1	0	0
Riverside County	3,268	0	0	0	0	0	0	0	0
Sacramento County	4,123	1	1	0	0	0	0	0	0
San Bernardino County	5,592	0	0	0	0	0	0	0	0
San Diego County[a]	5,172	12	0	10	1	/	/	/	/
San Luis Obispo County	503	0	0	0	0	0	0	0	0
Santa Clara County[a]	4,525	2	0	2	0	/	/	/	/
Santa Cruz County[a,d]	599	0	0	0	0	/	/	/	/
Sierra County	10	0	0	0	0	0	0	0	0
Solano County[a]	1,061	1	0	0	1	/	/	/	/
Stanislaus County	1,284	0	0	0	0	0	0	0	0
Colorado									
Adams County[a]	1,197	1	1	0	0	/	/	/	/
Denver City[a,d,e]	2,336	0	0	0	0	/	/	/	/
Gilpin County[a]	53	0	0	0	0	/	/	/	/
La Plata County[a]	175	0	0	0	0	/	/	/	/
Larimer County[a]	528	0	0	0	0	/	/	/	/
Mesa County[a]	365	0	0	0	0	/	/	/	/
Sedgwick County[b]	3	0	0	0	0	0	0	0	0
District of Columbia[c]	3,588	3	0	2	0	/	/	/	/
Florida									
Bradford County	226	0	0	0	0	0	0	0	0
Broward County[c,e]	5,482	3	0	0	3	/	/	/	/
Charlotte County	471	0	0	0	0	0	0	0	0
Dade County[a]	6,772	3	0	0	2	/	/	/	/
Hillsborough County[a]	4,637	0	0	0	0	/	/	/	/
Indian River County	627	0	0	0	0	0	0	0	0
Jacksonville City[a]	3,420	13	0	13	0	/	/	/	/
Orange County[a]	3,706	0	0	0	0	/	/	/	/
Palm Beach County	2,789	0	0	0	0	0	0	0	0

Appendix table 2a (continued). Allegations of inmate-on-inmate sexual violence reported by local jail authorities, by type, 2005

Jurisdiction and facility	Average daily population, 2005	Reported inmate-on-inmate nonconsensual sexual acts				Reported inmate-on-inmate abusive sexual contacts			
		Allega-tions	Sub-stantiated	Unsub-stantiated	Unfounded	Allega-tions	Sub-stantiated	Unsub-stantiated	Unfounded
Florida (continued)									
Pinellas County[a]	3,317	0	0	0	0	/	/	/	/
Polk County	2,724	4	1	1	2	0	0	0	0
St. Lucie County	1,073	0	0	0	0	0	0	0	0
Sarasota County[b]	873	0	0	0	0	0	0	0	0
Seminole County	933	0	0	0	0	1	0	1	0
Taylor County	123	0	0	0	0	0	0	0	0
Volusia County	1,575	0	0	0	0	4	2	1	1
Wakulla County	218	0	0	0	0	0	0	0	0
Georgia									
Augusta-Richmond County	1,087	0	0	0	0	0	0	0	0
Ben Hill County	116	0	0	0	0	0	0	0	0
Butts County	118	0	0	0	0	0	0	0	0
Carroll County Cor. Inst.	230	0	0	0	0	0	0	0	0
Carroll County[a]	478	0	0	0	0	/	/	/	/
Cobb County[a]	2,265	1	0	0	1	/	/	/	/
Decatur County	296	0	0	0	0	0	0	0	0
DeKalb County[a]	3,032	3	1	1	1	/	/	/	/
East Point City	62	0	0	0	0	0	0	0	0
Forsyth County	136	0	0	0	0	0	0	0	0
Fulton County[a]	3,200	17	/	/	/	/	/	/	/
Gwinnett County Cor. Inst.[a]	723	0	0	0	0	/	/	/	/
Gwinnett County	1,766	0	0	0	0	0	0	0	0
Lowndes County	645	0	0	0	0	0	0	0	0
Milledgeville City	4	0	0	0	0	0	0	0	0
Monroe County	128	0	0	0	0	0	0	0	0
Muscogee County[a,e]	598	0	0	0	0	/	/	/	/
Peach County	70	0	0	0	0	0	0	0	0
Polk County[a]	150	0	0	0	0	/	/	/	/
Taylor County[a]	27	0	0	0	0	/	/	/	/
Troup County[d]	428	0	0	0	0	0	0	0	0
Upson County	151	0	0	0	0	0	0	0	0
Idaho									
Adams County	25	0	0	0	0	0	0	0	0
Bingham County	111	0	0	0	0	0	0	0	0
Canyon County	579	1	0	1	0	0	0	0	0
Illinois									
Adams County	106	0	0	0	0	0	0	0	0
Cook County	9,854	12	0	8	2	0	0	0	0
Jackson County[a]	108	0	0	0	0	/	/	/	/
Jo Daviess County	25	0	0	0	0	0	0	0	0
Kankakee County	385	0	0	0	0	0	0	0	0
Stark County	6	0	0	0	0	0	0	0	0
Will County[a]	568	0	0	0	0	/	/	/	/
Woodford County	42	0	0	0	0	0	0	0	0
Indiana									
Clinton County[a]	118	0	0	0	0	/	/	/	/
Floyd County	273	15	10	2	3	/	/	/	/
Greene County[a]	83	0	0	0	0	/	/	/	/
Hendricks County	276	1	0	0	0	0	0	0	0
Lake County[a]	970	0	0	0	0	/	/	/	/
Marion County[a]	2,584	4	0	2	2	/	/	/	/
Perry County	38	0	0	0	0	0	0	0	0
Porter County[a]	493	4	0	4	0	/	/	/	/
Shelby County[a]	187	0	0	0	0	/	/	/	/
Tippecanoe County[a]	504	0	0	0	0	/	/	/	/
Vermillion County	78	0	0	0	0	0	0	0	0
Iowa									
Buchanan County	915	0	0	0	0	0	0	0	0
Davis County[a]	8	0	0	0	0	/	/	/	/
Fremont County	7	0	0	0	0	0	0	0	0
Linn County[c]	380	0	0	0	0	/	/	/	/
Marshall County	151	0	0	0	0	0	0	0	0
Mills County[a]	9	0	0	0	0	/	/	/	/
Polk County[a]	971	0	0	0	0	/	/	/	/

Jurisdiction and facility	Average daily population, 2005	Reported inmate-on-inmate nonconsensual sexual acts				Reported inmate-on-inmate abusive sexual contacts			
		Allega-tions	Sub-stantiated	Unsub-stantiated	Unfounded	Allega-tions	Sub-stantiated	Unsub-stantiated	Unfounded
Kansas									
Galena City	4	0	0	0	0	0	0	0	0
Geary County	79	0	0	0	0	0	0	0	0
Kingman County[a]	8	0	0	0	0	/	/	/	/
Ottawa County	59	0	0	0	0	0	0	0	0
Sedgwick County	1,501	1	0	0	1	3	0	1	0
Stevens County[a]	14	0	0	0	0	/	/	/	/
Kentucky									
Campbell County	294	0	0	0	0	0	0	0	0
Daviess County[a]	650	0	0	0	0	/	/	/	/
Hardin County	523	0	0	0	0	0	0	0	0
Laurel County	365	0	0	0	0	0	0	0	0
Louisville-Jefferson County[a]	1,830	1	0	0	1	/	/	/	/
Mason County	119	0	0	0	0	0	0	0	0
Meade County	142	0	0	0	0	0	0	0	0
Ohio County[a]	47	0	0	0	0	/	/	/	/
Oldham County[c,d]	90	0	0	0	0	/	/	/	/
Whitley County[f]	90	0	0	0	0	0	0	0	0
Louisiana									
Amite City	12	0	0	0	0	0	0	0	0
Avoyelles Parish	1,000	0	0	0	0	0	0	0	0
Calcasieu Parish	1,190	5	3	2	0	1	0	1	0
Iberia Parish[a]	450	0	0	0	0	/	/	/	/
Jennings City	41	0	0	0	0	0	0	0	0
Orleans Parish[a]	3,969	7	/	/	/	/	/	/	/
Ouachita Parish[a,e]	850	0	0	0	0	/	/	/	/
St. Charles Parish[a]	508	0	0	0	0	/	/	/	/
St. James Parish	91	0	0	0	0	0	0	0	0
St. Landry Parish	211	1	0	1	0	3	0	0	3
Terrebonne Parish[c]	616	0	0	0	0	/	/	/	/
Washington Parish	179	0	0	0	0	0	0	0	0
Maine									
Cumberland County	413	0	0	0	0	0	0	0	0
Oxford County[a]	44	0	0	0	0	/	/	/	/
Maryland									
Baltimore City	3,710	2	0	1	0	0	0	0	0
Montgomery County	978	0	0	0	0	0	0	0	0
Prince Georges County	1,256	1	0	0	1	0	0	0	0
St. Mary's County	306	2	1	0	0	0	0	0	0
Massachusetts									
Hampden County	1,607	0	0	0	0	1	1	0	0
Hampshire County	270	0	0	0	0	1	1	0	0
Middlesex County[a]	1,182	0	0	0	0	/	/	/	/
Plymouth County[a]	1,514	0	0	0	0	0	0	0	0
Michigan									
Delta County[a,d,e]	89	0	0	0	0	/	/	/	/
Dickson County	77	0	0	0	0	0	0	0	0
Genesee County	575	0	0	0	0	0	0	0	0
Jackson County	410	0	0	0	0	0	0	0	0
Kalkaska County[a]	47	0	0	0	0	/	/	/	/
Livingston County[a]	217	0	0	0	0	/	/	/	/
Mackinac County[a]	29	0	0	0	0	/	/	/	/
Macomb County	1,409	1	0	0	0	3	0	1	2
Monroe County	369	0	0	0	0	0	0	0	0
Van Buren County[a,d]	178	0	0	0	0	/	/	/	/
Wayne County	2,712	4	0	3	0	2	0	0	2
Minnesota									
Hennepin County	552	0	0	0	0	0	0	0	0
Houston County	12	0	0	0	0	0	0	0	0
Nicollet County	34	0	0	0	0	0	0	0	0
Winona County	41	0	0	0	0	0	0	0	0
Wright County	83	0	0	0	0	0	0	0	0
Mississippi									
Attalla County	32	0	0	0	0	0	0	0	0
Claiborne County	10	0	0	0	0	0	0	0	0
Harrison County[a,d]	925	0	0	0	0	/	/	/	/

Jurisdiction and facility	Average daily population, 2005	Reported inmate-on-inmate nonconsensual sexual acts				Reported inmate-on-inmate abusive sexual contacts			
		Allega-tions	Sub-stantiated	Unsub-stantiated	Unfounded	Allega-tions	Sub-stantiated	Unsub-stantiated	Unfounded
Mississippi (continued)									
Kemper-Neshoba County Regional	52	0	0	0	0	0	0	0	0
Leflore County	130	1	0	1	0	0	0	0	0
Stone County	344	0	0	0	0	0	0	0	0
Washington County	74	0	0	0	0	0	0	0	0
Wayne County[a]	49	0	0	0	0	/	/	/	/
Missouri									
Callaway County	76	0	0	0	0	0	0	0	0
Clinton County	22	0	0	0	0	0	0	0	0
Greene County	501	3	0	1	2	0	0	0	0
Howard County	12	0	0	0	0	0	0	0	0
Howell County	41	0	0	0	0	0	0	0	0
Kansas City	132	0	0	0	0	0	0	0	0
Phelps County	123	0	0	0	0	0	0	0	0
Reynolds County	3	0	0	0	0	0	0	0	0
St. Francois County[a]	136	1	0	1	0	/	/	/	/
St. Louis City[a]	1,572	0	0	0	0	/	/	/	/
Montana									
Glacier County[a,e]	5	0	0	0	0	/	/	/	/
Lake County	40	0	0	0	0	1	1	0	0
Yellowstone County[a,e]	430	1	1	0	0	/	/	/	/
Nebraska									
Cedar County	3	0	0	0	0	0	0	0	0
Douglas County[a]	1,034	0	0	0	0	/	/	/	/
Fillmore County[a,d,e]	3	0	0	0	0	/	/	/	/
Seward County[a]	23	0	0	0	0	/	/	/	/
Nevada									
Clark County	3,296	0	0	0	0	1	1	0	0
Lander County	22	0	0	0	0	0	0	0	0
Washoe County	1,077	0	0	0	0	1	1	0	0
New Hampshire									
Hillsborough County	524	1	0	0	1	0	0	0	0
Merrimack County[a]	180	0	0	0	0	/	/	/	/
New Jersey									
Bergen County	989	0	0	0	0	0	0	0	0
Essex County	2,138	2	0	0	2	2	0	0	2
Hudson County	2,064	3	/	/	/	3	0	0	3
Middlesex County	1,152	2	0	0	0	0	0	0	0
Ocean County[a]	471	1	0	0	0	/	/	/	/
Salem County	270	0	0	0	0	0	0	0	0
New Mexico									
Bernalillo County	2,239	8	1	2	4	2	0	0	1
Lea County	289	0	0	0	0	0	0	0	0
Rio Arriba County[a]	120	0	0	0	0	/	/	/	/
San Juan County	598	0	0	0	0	2	0	2	0
Sierra County	60	0	0	0	0	0	0	0	0
New York									
Erie County Holding Center	714	1	0	0	1	0	0	0	0
Livingston County	100	0	0	0	0	0	0	0	0
Nassau County[e]	1,581	2	0	0	1	0	0	0	0
New York City[a]	13,420	6	0	4	2	/	/	/	/
Onondaga County	672	0	0	0	0	0	0	0	0
Oswego County	145	0	0	0	0	0	0	0	0
Rensselaer County[a]	320	0	0	0	0	/	/	/	/
Steuben County	162	0	0	0	0	0	0	0	0
North Carolina									
Alamance County[a]	276	0	0	0	0	/	/	/	/
Beaufort County	88	0	0	0	0	0	0	0	0
Cumberland County	511	0	0	0	0	1	0	0	1
Dare County	113	0	0	0	0	0	0	0	0
Greene County[a]	73	0	0	0	0	/	/	/	/
Harnett County	145	0	0	0	0	/	/	/	/
Mecklenburg County[a]	2,178	1	0	0	1	/	/	/	/
New Hanover County[a]	517	1	0	0	1	/	/	/	/
Randolph County[a]	200	0	0	0	0	/	/	/	/
Wake County	1,682	0	0	0	0	0	0	0	0

Appendix table 2a (continued). Allegations of inmate-on-inmate sexual violence reported by local jail authorities, by type, 2005

Jurisdiction and facility	Average daily population, 2005	Reported inmate-on-inmate nonconsensual sexual acts				Reported inmate-on-inmate abusive sexual contacts			
		Allega-tions	Sub-stantiated	Unsub-stantiated	Unfounded	Allega-tions	Sub-stantiated	Unsub-stantiated	Unfounded
North Dakota									
Cass County	223	0	0	0	0	0	0	0	0
Grand Forks County	113	0	0	0	0	0	0	0	0
Mercer County	25	0	0	0	0	0	0	0	0
Ohio									
Ashland County[a]	95	0	0	0	0	/	/	/	/
Brown County	46	0	0	0	0	0	0	0	0
Butler County[a]	766	0	0	0	0	/	/	/	/
Carroll County	41	0	0	0	0	0	0	0	0
Clark County[a]	227	0	0	0	0	/	/	/	/
Franklin County	2,370	0	0	0	0	0	0	0	0
Greene County[a]	370	0	0	0	0	/	/	/	/
Hamilton County	2,101	1	1	0	0	1	1	0	0
Highland Heights City	1	0	0	0	0	0	0	0	0
Mahoning County	428	0	0	0	0	0	0	0	0
Muskingum County	169	0	0	0	0	0	0	0	0
Richland County	133	0	0	0	0	0	0	0	0
Oklahoma									
Coal County	15	0	0	0	0	0	0	0	0
Comanche County[a]	230	0	0	0	0	/	/	/	/
Custer County[a]	75	0	0	0	0	/	/	/	/
Eufaula City[a]	3	0	0	0	0	/	/	/	/
Johnston County	41	0	0	0	0	0	0	0	0
Le Flore County[b,e]	67	0	0	0	0	0	0	0	0
Oklahoma County[a]	2,800	5	0	0	5	/	/	/	/
Okmulgee County[a]	140	0	0	0	0	/	/	/	/
Oregon									
Deschutes County	231	0	0	0	0	0	0	0	0
Josephine County	130	0	0	0	0	0	0	0	0
Lane County	572	0	0	0	0	0	0	0	0
Multnomah County[a]	1,495	0	0	0	0	/	/	/	/
Pennsylvania									
Allegheny County	2,394	0	0	0	0	0	0	0	0
Cumberland County[d]	350	0	0	0	0	0	0	0	0
Dauphin County	1,265	4	0	0	4	0	0	0	0
Greene County[a]	112	0	0	0	0	/	/	/	/
Lebanon County	449	0	0	0	0	0	0	0	0
Luzerne County	753	0	0	0	0	0	0	0	0
Montgomery County	1,543	2	0	0	2	0	0	0	0
Philadelphia City	7,792	5	2	2	1	1	0	1	0
Pike County	279	0	0	0	0	0	0	0	0
Union County[d]	60	0	0	0	0	0	0	0	0
South Carolina									
Beaufort County	243	0	0	0	0	0	0	0	0
Charleston County	1,466	7	0	0	0	1	0	0	0
Edgefield County[a]	34	0	0	0	0	/	/	/	/
Lexington County[a,d,e]	609	2	0	2	0	/	/	/	/
Pickens County[c]	98	0	0	0	0	/	/	/	/
Sumter-Lee County Regional[a]	393	0	0	0	0	/	/	/	/
South Dakota									
Charles Mix County[a]	34	0	0	0	0	/	/	/	/
Minnehaha County[a]	560	1	0	0	0	/	/	/	/
Tennessee									
De Kalb County	82	0	0	0	0	0	0	0	0
Dickson County	203	0	0	0	0	0	0	0	0
Fentress County	47	0	0	0	0	0	0	0	0
Greene County	294	0	0	0	0	0	0	0	0
Knox County	1,052	0	0	0	0	0	0	0	0
Lincoln County[c]	112	0	0	0	0	/	/	/	/
Nashville-Davidson County	2,250	2	0	2	0	1	0	1	0
Rhea County	114	1	0	0	0	0	0	0	0
Scott County	46	0	0	0	0	0	0	0	0
She by County[a]	2,519	2	0	0	2	/	/	/	/
Sullivan County[a]	575	1	0	0	0	/	/	/	/

Appendix table 2a (continued). Allegations of inmate-on-inmate sexual violence reported by local jail authorities, by type, 2005

Jurisdiction and facility	Average daily population, 2005	Reported inmate-on-inmate nonconsensual sexual acts				Reported inmate-on-inmate abusive sexual contacts			
		Allega-tions	Sub-stantiated	Unsub-stantiated	Unfounded	Allega-tions	Sub-stantiated	Unsub-stantiated	Unfounded
Texas									
Bell County	645	0	0	0	0	0	0	0	0
Bexar County	3,871	0	0	0	0	0	0	0	0
Brown County[a]	155	0	0	0	0	/	/	/	/
Burleson County	60	0	0	0	0	0	0	0	0
Cameron County	968	0	0	0	0	0	0	0	0
Comal County[a]	263	0	0	0	0	/	/	/	/
Crane County[a]	12	0	0	0	0	/	/	/	/
Dallas County[a]	7,629	5	2	0	3	/	/	/	/
El Paso County	2,110	1	1	0	0	0	0	0	0
Falls County[a]	93	0	0	0	0	/	/	/	/
Fort Bend County	835	0	0	0	0	0	0	0	0
Galveston County	882	0	0	0	0	0	0	0	0
Grayson County[a]	463	0	0	0	0	/	/	/	/
Gregg County	512	0	0	0	0	0	0	0	0
Hale County[a]	118	0	0	0	0	/	/	/	/
Harris County	8,730	13	1	3	5	1	0	0	1
Hutchison County[a]	57	0	0	0	0	/	/	/	/
Johnson County[a]	480	0	0	0	0	/	/	/	/
Kemah City	1	0	0	0	0	0	0	0	0
Lamar County	174	0	0	0	0	0	0	0	0
Live Oak County	25	0	0	0	0	0	0	0	0
Lubbock County	731	4	0	0	4	2	0	0	2
Medina County	85	1	1	0	0	0	0	0	0
Robertson County	28	0	0	0	0	0	0	0	0
Tarrant County[a]	3,299	0	0	0	0	/	/	/	/
Travis County[a]	2,629	10	2	3	2	/	/	/	/
Zavala County	63	0	0	0	0	0	0	0	0
Utah									
Carbon County	76	0	0	0	0	0	0	0	0
Rich County	1	0	0	0	0	0	0	0	0
Salt Lake County	1,913	0	0	0	0	1	0	0	1
Washington County[a]	450	1	0	1	0	/	/	/	/
Virginia									
A bemarle-Charlottesville Regional	446	1	1	0	0	0	0	0	0
Augusta County[a]	223	0	0	0	0	/	/	/	/
Henrico County	1,143	2	0	1	1	0	0	0	0
Loudon County	155	0	0	0	0	0	0	0	0
Newport News City[a]	656	0	0	0	0	/	/	/	/
Norfolk City	1,664	1	0	0	1	0	0	0	0
Pamunkey Regional	411	0	0	0	0	0	0	0	0
Rappahannock Regional[a]	964	1	0	0	1	/	/	/	/
Richmond City	1,378	0	0	0	0	0	0	0	0
Shenandoah County	75	0	0	0	0	0	0	0	0
Virginia Peninsula Regional	381	0	0	0	0	0	0	0	0
Warren County[a]	119	1	1	0	0	/	/	/	/
Washington									
King County[a]	2,303	0	0	0	0	/	/	/	/
Pacific County	34	0	0	0	0	0	0	0	0
Pierce County[a]	1,298	0	0	0	0	/	/	/	/
Spokane County[a]	621	1	0	1	0	/	/	/	/
Thurston County[a]	432	4	0	1	3	/	/	/	/
Whatcom County[a]	263	0	0	0	0	/	/	/	/
West Virginia									
Kanawha County Regional	486	0	0	0	0	0	0	0	0
Raleigh County Regional[a]	459	2	0	1	1	/	/	/	/

Appendix table 2a (continued). Allegations of inmate-on-inmate sexual violence reported by local jail authorities, by type, 2005

Jurisdiction and facility	Average daily population, 2005	Reported inmate-on-inmate nonconsensual sexual acts				Reported inmate-on-inmate abusive sexual contacts			
		Allega-tions	Sub-stantiated	Unsub-stantiated	Unfounded	Allega-tions	Sub-stantiated	Unsub-stantiated	Unfounded
Wisconsin									
Marathon County	293	0	0	0	0	1	1	0	0
Milwaukee County	863	1	0	1	0	0	0	0	0
Milwaukee County House of Cor.[a]	2,327	0	0	0	0	/	/	/	/
Polk County	108	0	0	0	0	0	0	0	0
Richland County	27	1	0	0	1	1	1	0	0
Sawyer County	30	0	0	0	0	0	0	0	0
Washington County	202	0	0	0	0	1	0	1	0
Waukesha County	563	0	0	0	0	3	0	0	3
Wyoming									
A bany County[c,f]	73	0	0	0	0	/	/	/	/
Converse County[a]	35	0	0	0	0	/	/	/	/
Natrona County[a]	305	1	0	0	1	/	/	/	/

Note: The total number of allegations includes ongoing investigations (not shown).

/Not reported.

[a]Allegations of abusive sexual contacts could not be counted separately from allegations of nonconsensual sexual acts.

[b]Number of inmates confined on December 31, 2005.

[c]Reports of abusive sexual contacts are not recorded in a central database.

[d]Allegations limited to substantiated occurrences only.

[e]Allegations limited to completed acts only.

[f]Number of inmates confined on June 30, 2005.

Appendix table 2b. Allegations of staff sexual misconduct with inmates reported by local jail authorities, by type, 2005

	Reported allegations of staff sexual misconduct with inmates				Reported allegations of staff sexual harassment of inmates			
	Allegations	Sub-stantiated	Unsub-stantiated	Unfounded	Allegations	Sub-stantiated	Unsub-stantiated	Unfounded
Total	184	53	50	42	39	3	12	15
Alabama								
Attalla City	0	0	0	0	0	0	0	0
Autauga County	0	0	0	0	0	0	0	0
Bibb County[a]	0	0	0	0	/	/	/	/
Chilton County	0	0	0	0	0	0	0	0
Crenshaw County[a]	0	0	0	0	/	/	/	/
Franklin County	1	1	0	0	0	0	0	0
Lipscomb City	0	0	0	0	0	0	0	0
Madison County	1	0	0	0	0	0	0	0
Mobile County	0	0	0	0	2	0	2	0
Pickens County	0	0	0	0	0	0	0	0
Pleasant Grove City	0	0	0	0	0	0	0	0
Russell County	0	0	0	0	0	0	0	0
Alaska								
Unalaska City[b]	0	0	0	0	/	/	/	/
Arizona								
Maricopa County	9	1	4	3	0	0	0	0
Mohave County	0	0	0	0	0	0	0	0
Pinal County[a]	0	0	0	0	/	/	/	/
Arkansas								
Brinkley City	0	0	0	0	0	0	0	0
Craighead County[a,c]	0	0	0	0	/	/	/	/
Dallas County[b,d]	/	/	/	/	/	/	/	/
Drew County	0	0	0	0	1	0	0	1
Pulaski County Regional	0	0	0	0	0	0	0	0
Warren City	0	0	0	0	0	0	0	0
California								
Calaveras County	0	0	0	0	0	0	0	0
Contra Costa County[a]	0	0	0	0	/	/	/	/
Fresno County	0	0	0	0	4	0	2	0
Kern County	2	0	2	0	0	0	0	0
Kings County	0	0	0	0	0	0	0	0
Los Angeles County	1	0	1	0	0	0	0	0
Nevada County	0	0	0	0	0	0	0	0
Orange County	0	0	0	0	0	0	0	0
Riverside County	0	0	0	0	0	0	0	0
Sacramento County	0	0	0	0	0	0	0	0
San Bernardino County	0	0	0	0	0	0	0	0
San Diego County	2	0	2	0	1	0	0	1
San Luis Obispo County	0	0	0	0	0	0	0	0
Santa Clara County	2	0	0	0	0	0	0	0
Santa Cruz County	1	0	1	0	0	0	0	0
Sierra County	0	0	0	0	0	0	0	0
Solano County	0	0	0	0	1	1	0	0
Stanislaus County[a,c]	0	0	0	0	/	/	/	/
Colorado								
Adams County	1	0	0	1	0	0	0	0
Denver City[a]	0	0	0	0	/	/	/	/
Gilpin County[a]	0	0	0	0	/	/	/	/
La Plata County	0	0	0	0	0	0	0	0
Larimer County	2	0	2	0	1	0	1	0
Mesa County	0	0	0	0	0	0	0	0
Sedgwick County[a]	0	0	0	0	/	/	/	/
District of Columbia	3	0	1	1	1	0	0	0
Florida								
Bradford County	0	0	0	0	0	0	0	0
Broward County[b]	10	1	1	6	/	/	/	/
Charlotte County	1	0	0	1	0	0	0	0
Dade County	0	0	0	0	5	0	1	2
Hillsborough County[a]	2	2	0	0	/	/	/	/
Indian River County	0	0	0	0	0	0	0	0
Jacksonville City	0	0	0	0	1	0	0	0
Orange County	0	0	0	0	0	0	0	0
Palm Beach County	0	0	0	0	0	0	0	0
Pinellas County	1	0	0	1	1	0	1	0
Polk County	1	0	0	1	0	0	0	0

Appendix table 2b (continued). Allegations of staff sexual misconduct with inmates reported by local jail authorities, by type, 2005

	Reported allegations of staff sexual misconduct with inmates				Reported allegations of staff sexual harassment of inmates			
	Allegations	Sub-stantiated	Unsub-stantiated	Unfounded	Allegations	Sub-stantiated	Unsub-stantiated	Unfounded
Florida (continued)								
Sarasota County	0	0	0	0	0	0	0	0
Seminole County	1	0	1	0	0	0	0	0
St. Lucie County	0	0	0	0	0	0	0	0
Taylor County	0	0	0	0	0	0	0	0
Volusia County	0	0	0	0	0	0	0	0
Wakulla County	0	0	0	0	0	0	0	0
Georgia								
Augusta-Richmond County	0	0	0	0	0	0	0	0
Ben Hill County	0	0	0	0	0	0	0	0
Butts County	0	0	0	0	0	0	0	0
Carroll County Cor. Inst.	0	0	0	0	0	0	0	0
Carroll County[a]	0	0	0	0	/	/	/	/
Cobb County	0	0	0	0	0	0	0	0
Decatur County	0	0	0	0	0	0	0	0
DeKalb County[a]	3	1	1	1	/	/	/	/
East Point City	0	0	0	0	0	0	0	0
Forsyth County	0	0	0	0	0	0	0	0
Fulton County	/	/	/	/	/	/	/	/
Gwinnett County Cor. Inst.	0	0	0	0	1	0	0	1
Gwinnett County	0	0	0	0	0	0	0	0
Lowndes County	0	0	0	0	0	0	0	0
Milledgeville City	0	0	0	0	0	0	0	0
Monroe County	0	0	0	0	0	0	0	0
Muscogee County[a,c]	0	0	0	0	/	/	/	/
Peach County	0	0	0	0	0	0	0	0
Po k County[a]	0	0	0	0	/	/	/	/
Taylor County[a]	0	0	0	0	/	/	/	/
Troup County	0	0	0	0	0	0	0	0
Upson County[a]	0	0	0	0	/	/	/	/
Idaho								
Adams County	0	0	0	0	0	0	0	0
Bingham County	0	0	0	0	0	0	0	0
Canyon County	0	0	0	0	0	0	0	0
Illinois								
Adams County	0	0	0	0	0	0	0	0
Cook County	1	0	0	0	0	0	0	0
Jackson County	0	0	0	0	0	0	0	0
Jo Daviess County	0	0	0	0	0	0	0	0
Kankakee County	0	0	0	0	0	0	0	0
Stark County	0	0	0	0	0	0	0	0
Will County[a]	0	0	0	0	/	/	/	/
Woodford County	0	0	0	0	0	0	0	0
Indiana								
Clinton County[a]	0	0	0	0	/	/	/	/
Floyd County[a]	0	0	0	0	/	/	/	/
Greene County[a]	0	0	0	0	/	/	/	/
Hendricks County	1	0	1	0	0	0	0	0
Lake County	0	0	0	0	0	0	0	0
Marion County	0	0	0	0	0	0	0	0
Perry County	0	0	0	0	0	0	0	0
Porter County[d]	/	/	/	/	1	0	0	1
Shelby County[a]	1	1	0	0	/	/	/	/
Tippecanoe County[a]	1	1	0	0	/	/	/	/
Vermillion County	0	0	0	0	0	0	0	0
Iowa								
Buchanan County	0	0	0	0	0	0	0	0
Davis County	0	0	0	0	0	0	0	0
Fremont County	0	0	0	0	0	0	0	0
Linn County[a]	0	0	0	0	/	/	/	/
Marshall County	0	0	0	0	0	0	0	0
Mills County[a]	0	0	0	0	/	/	/	/
Po k County	0	0	0	0	0	0	0	0

Appendix table 2b (continued). Allegations of staff sexual misconduct with inmates reported by local jail authorities, by type, 2005

	Reported allegations of staff sexual misconduct with inmates				Reported allegations of staff sexual harassment of inmates			
	Allegations	Sub-stantiated	Unsub-stantiated	Unfounded	Allegations	Sub-stantiated	Unsub-stantiated	Unfounded
Kansas								
Galena City	0	0	0	0	0	0	0	0
Geary County	0	0	0	0	0	0	0	0
Kingman County	0	0	0	0	0	0	0	0
Ottawa County	0	0	0	0	0	0	0	0
Sedgwick County	2	1	0	1	0	0	0	0
Stevens County[a]	0	0	0	0	/	/	/	/
Kentucky								
Campbell County	0	0	0	0	0	0	0	0
Daviess County	0	0	0	0	0	0	0	0
Hardin County[a]	0	0	0	0	/	/	/	/
Laurel County	0	0	0	0	0	0	0	0
Louisville-Jefferson County[a]	2	0	0	2	/	/	/	/
Mason County	0	0	0	0	0	0	0	0
Meade County	0	0	0	0	0	0	0	0
Ohio County[a]	0	0	0	0	/	/	/	/
Oldham County[c]	0	0	0	0	0	0	0	0
Whitley County	0	0	0	0	0	0	0	0
Louisiana								
Amite City[a]	0	0	0	0	/	/	/	/
Avoyelles Parish	0	0	0	0	0	0	0	0
Calcasieu Parish	3	3	0	0	0	0	0	0
Iberia Parish[a]	0	0	0	0	/	/	/	/
Jennings City	0	0	0	0	0	0	0	0
Orleans Parish[a]	/	/	/	/	/	/	/	/
Ouachita Parish[a]	0	0	0	0	/	/	/	/
St. Charles Parish	0	0	0	0	0	0	0	0
St. James Parish[a]	0	0	0	0	/	/	/	/
St. Landry Parish	0	0	0	0	0	0	0	0
Terrebonne Parish	0	0	0	0	0	0	0	0
Washington Paris[a]	0	0	0	0	/	/	/	/
Maine								
Cumberland County	0	0	0	0	0	0	0	0
Oxford County	0	0	0	0	0	0	0	0
Maryland								
Baltimore City	1	0	1	0	0	0	0	0
Montgomery County	1	1	0	0	0	0	0	0
Prince Georges County	1	0	1	0	0	0	0	0
St. Mary's County	0	0	0	0	0	0	0	0
Massachusetts								
Hampden County[a]	0	0	0	0	/	/	/	/
Hampshire County	0	0	0	0	0	0	0	0
Middlesex County	0	0	0	0	0	0	0	0
Plymouth County[a,c]	0	0	0	0	/	/	/	/
Michigan								
Delta County[a]	0	0	0	0	/	/	/	/
Dickson County	0	0	0	0	0	0	0	0
Genesee County	0	0	0	0	0	0	0	0
Jackson County	1	1	0	0	0	0	0	0
Kalkaska County	1	0	0	1	0	0	0	0
Livingston County[a]	0	0	0	0	/	/	/	/
Mackinac County	0	0	0	0	0	0	0	0
Macomb County	0	0	0	0	0	0	0	0
Monroe County	0	0	0	0	0	0	0	0
Van Buren County[a,c]	0	0	0	0	/	/	/	/
Wayne County	0	0	0	0	0	0	0	0
Minnesota								
Hennepin County	1	0	1	0	0	0	0	0
Houston County	0	0	0	0	0	0	0	0
Nicollet County[a]	1	0	1	0	/	/	/	/
Winona County	0	0	0	0	0	0	0	0
Wright County	0	0	0	0	0	0	0	0

Appendix table 2b (continued). Allegations of staff sexual misconduct with inmates reported by local jail authorities, by type, 2005

	Reported allegations of staff sexual misconduct with inmates				Reported allegations of staff sexual harassment of inmates			
	Allegations	Sub-stantiated	Unsub-stantiated	Unfounded	Allegations	Sub-stantiated	Unsub-stantiated	Unfounded
Mississippi								
Attalla County	0	0	0	0	0	0	0	0
Claiborne County	0	0	0	0	0	0	0	0
Harrison County[a,c]	1	1	0	0	/	/	/	/
Kemper-Neshoba County Regional[a]	1	1	0	0	/	/	/	/
Leflore County	0	0	0	0	0	0	0	0
Stone County	0	0	0	0	0	0	0	0
Washington County	0	0	0	0	0	0	0	0
Wayne County	0	0	0	0	0	0	0	0
Missouri								
Callaway County	0	0	0	0	0	0	0	0
Clinton County	0	0	0	0	0	0	0	0
Greene County	1	1	0	0	0	0	0	0
Howard County	0	0	0	0	0	0	0	0
Howell County	0	0	0	0	0	0	0	0
Kansas City	0	0	0	0	1	0	1	0
Phelps County	0	0	0	0	0	0	0	0
Reynolds County	0	0	0	0	0	0	0	0
St. Francois County	0	0	0	0	0	0	0	0
St. Louis City	0	0	0	0	0	0	0	0
Montana								
Glacier County[c]	0	0	0	0	0	0	0	0
Lake County	0	0	0	0	0	0	0	0
Yellowstone County[a]	0	0	0	0	/	/	/	/
Nebraska								
Cedar County	0	0	0	0	0	0	0	0
Douglas County	0	0	0	0	0	0	0	0
Fillmore County[c]	0	0	0	0	0	0	0	0
Seward County[a]	0	0	0	0	/	/	/	/
Nevada								
Clark County	1	0	0	1	0	0	0	0
Lander County	0	0	0	0	0	0	0	0
Washoe County	2	0	0	2	0	0	0	0
New Hampshire								
Hillsborough County	0	0	0	0	0	0	0	0
Merrimack County[a]	5	0	5	0	/	/	/	/
New Jersey								
Bergen County	0	0	0	0	0	0	0	0
Essex County	0	0	0	0	0	0	0	0
Hudson County	1	1	0	0	0	0	0	0
Middlesex County	1	0	0	1	0	0	0	0
Ocean County	2	0	0	0	0	0	0	0
Salem County	1	0	0	1	1	0	0	1
New Mexico								
Bernalillo County[b]	4	2	0	1	/	/	/	/
Lea County[a]	0	0	0	0	/	/	/	/
Rio Arriba County	0	0	0	0	0	0	0	0
San Juan County	0	0	0	0	0	0	0	0
Sierra County	0	0	0	0	0	0	0	0
New York								
Erie County Holding Center	3	0	0	2	0	0	0	0
Livingston County	0	0	0	0	0	0	0	0
Nassau County	0	0	0	0	1	0	0	0
New York City[a]	25	2	9	2	/	/	/	/
Onondaga County	1	1	0	0	1	0	0	1
Oswego County	0	0	0	0	0	0	0	0
Rensselaer County	2	2	0	0	0	0	0	0
Steuben County	0	0	0	0	0	0	0	0
North Carolina								
Alamance County	0	0	0	0	0	0	0	0
Beaufort County[a]	0	0	0	0	/	/	/	/
Cumberland County	0	0	0	0	1	0	0	1
Dare County	0	0	0	0	0	0	0	0
Greene County[a]	0	0	0	0	/	/	/	/

	Reported allegations of staff sexual misconduct with inmates				Reported allegations of staff sexual harassment of inmates			
	Allegations	Sub-stantiated	Unsub-stantiated	Unfounded	Allegations	Sub-stantiated	Unsub-stantiated	Unfounded
North Carolina (continued)								
Harnett County	0	0	0	0	0	0	0	0
Mecklenburg County[a]	0	0	0	0	/	/	/	/
New Hanover County[a]	0	0	0	0	/	/	/	/
Randolph County[a]	0	0	0	0	/	/	/	/
Wake County	0	0	0	0	0	0	0	0
North Dakota								
Cass County	1	0	1	0	0	0	0	0
Grand Forks County	0	0	0	0	0	0	0	0
Mercer County	0	0	0	0	0	0	0	0
Ohio								
Ashland County	0	0	0	0	0	0	0	0
Brown County	0	0	0	0	0	0	0	0
Butler County[a]	0	0	0	0	/	/	/	/
Carroll County	0	0	0	0	0	0	0	0
Clark County	0	0	0	0	0	0	0	0
Franklin County	1	1	0	0	0	0	0	0
Greene County[a]	0	0	0	0	/	/	/	/
Hamilton County	1	1	0	0	0	0	0	0
Highland Heights City	0	0	0	0	0	0	0	0
Mahoning County	0	0	0	0	0	0	0	0
Muskingum County	1	0	0	1	0	0	0	0
Richland County	0	0	0	0	0	0	0	0
Oklahoma								
Coal County	0	0	0	0	0	0	0	0
Comanche County[c]	0	0	0	0	0	0	0	0
Custer County	0	0	0	0	0	0	0	0
Eufaula City[a]	0	0	0	0	/	/	/	/
Johnston County	0	0	0	0	0	0	0	0
Le Flore County	0	0	0	0	0	0	0	0
Oklahoma County	0	0	0	0	0	0	0	0
Okmulgee County	0	0	0	0	0	0	0	0
Oregon								
Deschutes County[a]	0	0	0	0	/	/	/	/
Josephine County	0	0	0	0	0	0	0	0
Lane County	0	0	0	0	1	0	0	1
Multnomah County[a]	0	0	0	0	/	/	/	/
Pennsylvania								
Allegheny County	0	0	0	0	0	0	0	0
Cumberland County[c]	0	0	0	0	0	0	0	0
Dauphin County	1	0	0	1	0	0	0	0
Greene County	0	0	0	0	0	0	0	0
Lebanon County	0	0	0	0	0	0	0	0
Luzerne County	0	0	0	0	0	0	0	0
Montgomery County	0	0	0	0	0	0	0	0
Philadelphia City	12	7	1	0	1	0	1	0
Pike County	0	0	0	0	0	0	0	0
Union County	0	0	0	0	0	0	0	0
South Carolina								
Beaufort County	1	0	1	0	0	0	0	0
Charleston County	3	2	1	0	0	0	0	0
Edgefield County	0	0	0	0	0	0	0	0
Lexington County	0	0	0	0	0	0	0	0
Pickens County	0	0	0	0	0	0	0	0
Sumter-Lee County Regional	0	0	0	0	0	0	0	0
South Dakota								
Charles Mix County[a]	0	0	0	0	/	/	/	/
Minnehaha County[a]	0	0	0	0	/	/	/	/
Tennessee								
De Kalb County	0	0	0	0	0	0	0	0
Dickson County	0	0	0	0	0	0	0	0
Fentress County	0	0	0	0	0	0	0	0
Greene County	0	0	0	0	1	0	0	1

Appendix table 2b (continued). Allegations of staff sexual misconduct with inmates reported by local jail authorities, by type, 2005							
	Reported allegations of staff sexual misconduct with inmates				Reported allegations of staff sexual harassment of inmates			
	Allegations	Sub-stantiated	Unsub-stantiated	Unfounded	Allegations	Sub-stantiated	Unsub-stantiated	Unfounded
Tennessee (continued								
Knox County[a]	1	1	0	0	/	/	/	/
Lincoln County	0	0	0	0	0	0	0	0
Nashville-Davidson County	6	1	4	1	0	0	0	0
Rhea County	0	0	0	0	1	0	0	0
Scott County	0	0	0	0	0	0	0	0
She by County	0	0	0	0	3	0	3	0
Sullivan County[a]	0	0	0	0	/	/	/	/
Texas								
Bell County	0	0	0	0	0	0	0	0
Bexar County	0	0	0	0	0	0	0	0
Brown County[a,c]	0	0	0	0	/	/	/	/
Burleson County	0	0	0	0	0	0	0	0
Cameron County	0	0	0	0	0	0	0	0
Comal County	0	0	0	0	0	0	0	0
Crane County[a]	0	0	0	0	/	/	/	/
Dallas County[a]	0	0	0	0	/	/	/	/
El Paso County	0	0	0	0	0	0	0	0
Falls County	0	0	0	0	0	0	0	0
Fort Bend County	0	0	0	0	0	0	0	0
Galveston County	0	0	0	0	0	0	0	0
Grayson County	0	0	0	0	0	0	0	0
Gregg County	1	0	0	1	0	0	0	0
Hale County[a]	0	0	0	0	/	/	/	/
Harris County	0	0	0	0	0	0	0	0
Hutchison County[a]	0	0	0	0	/	/	/	/
Johnson County	1	0	0	1	0	0	0	0
Kemah City	0	0	0	0	0	0	0	0
Lamar County	0	0	0	0	0	0	0	0
Live Oak County	0	0	0	0	0	0	0	0
Lubbock County	2	0	0	2	0	0	0	0
Medina County	0	0	0	0	0	0	0	0
Robertson County	0	0	0	0	0	0	0	0
Tarrant County[a]	3	1	1	0	/	/	/	/
Travis County	4	1	1	1	0	0	0	0
Zavala County	0	0	0	0	0	0	0	0
Utah								
Carbon County[a]	0	0	0	0	/	/	/	/
Rich County	0	0	0	0	0	0	0	0
Salt Lake County	15	10	0	3	1	1	0	0
Washington County	1	0	0	1	2	0	0	2
Virginia								
Albemarle-Charlottesville Regional	3	1	2	0	0	0	0	0
Augusta County[a]	0	0	0	0	/	/	/	/
Henrico County	4	0	1	1	0	0	0	0
Loudon County	0	0	0	0	0	0	0	0
Newport News City[a]	0	0	0	0	/	/	/	/
Norfo k City	0	0	0	0	0	0	0	0
Pamunkey Regional	1	1	0	0	0	0	0	0
Rappahannock Regional	0	0	0	0	0	0	0	0
Richmond City	0	0	0	0	0	0	0	0
Shenandoah County	0	0	0	0	1	0	0	1
Virginia Peninsula Regional	0	0	0	0	1	/	/	/
Warren County	0	0	0	0	0	0	0	0

Appendix table 2b (continued). Allegations of staff sexual misconduct with inmates reported by local jail authorities, by type, 2005

	Reported allegations of staff sexual misconduct with inmates				Reported allegations of staff sexual harassment of inmates			
	Allegations	Sub-stantiated	Unsub-stantiated	Unfounded	Allegations	Sub-stantiated	Unsub-stantiated	Unfounded
Washington								
King County	5	1	1	0	1	1	0	0
Pacific County	0	0	0	0	0	0	0	0
Pierce County[a]	0	0	0	0	/	/	/	/
Spokane County	0	0	0	0	0	0	0	0
Thurston County	0	0	0	0	0	0	0	0
Whatcom County	0	0	0	0	0	0	0	0
West Virgina								
Kanawha County Regional	1	0	0	0	1	0	0	1
Raleigh County Regional[a]	0	0	0	0	/	/	/	/
Wisconsin								
Marathon County[a]	0	0	0	0	/	/	/	/
Milwaukee County	1	0	0	0	0	0	0	0
Milwaukee County House of Cor.[a]	0	0	0	0	/	/	/	/
Po k County	0	0	0	0	0	0	0	0
Richland County	0	0	0	0	0	0	0	0
Sawyer County	0	0	0	0	0	0	0	0
Washington County	0	0	0	0	0	0	0	0
Waukesha County	1	0	1	0	0	0	0	0
Wyoming								
A bany County[b,d]	/	/	/	/	/	/	/	/
Converse County[b]	0	0	0	0	/	/	/	/
Natrona County[a]	0	0	0	0	/	/	/	/

Note: The total number of allegations includes ongoing investigations (not shown).
/Not reported.
[a]Reports of staff sexual misconduct may include reports of staff sexual harassment.
[b]Reports of staff sexual harassment are not recorded in a central database.
[c]Reports of staff sexual misconduct are based on substantiated allegations only.
[d]Reports of staff sexual misconduct are not recorded in a central database.

Appendix table 3a. Allegations of inmate-on-inmate sexual violence reported in private prisons and jails, by type, 2005

Jurisdiction and facility	Average daily population, 2005	Reported inmate-on-inmate nonconsensual sexual acts				Reported inmate-on-inmate abusive sexual contacts			
		Allega-tions	Sub-stantiated	Unsub-stantiated	Unfounded	Allega-tions	Sub-stantiated	Unsub-stantiated	Unfounded
Total	42,966	34	7	13	2	3	0	3	0
Arizona									
Arizona State Prison- Kingman (MTC)[a]	1,022	0	0	0	0	/	/	/	/
Central Arizona Detention Center (CCA)	3,259	0	0	0	0	1	0	1	0
California									
Central Valley Community Cor. (GEO)[a]	532	0	0	0	0	/	/	/	/
Taft Correctional Institution (GEO)	2,293	1	1	0	0	0	0	0	0
Colorado									
ComCor, Inc.[a]	456	0	0	0	0	/	/	/	/
Crowley County Correctional Facility (CSC)	920	0	0	0	0	0	0	0	0
Phoenix Center	201	0	0	0	0	0	0	0	0
Connecticut									
Cochegan House (Connections)	16	0	0	0	0	0	0	0	0
Florida									
Bay County Jail and Annex (CCA)	850	1	0	1	0	0	0	0	0
Moore Haven Correctional Facility (GEO)	747	0	0	0	0	0	0	0	0
South Bay Correctional Facility (GEO)	1,462	0	0	0	0	0	0	0	0
Georgia									
Wheeler Correctional Facility (CCA)	1,500	13	1	0	0	1	0	1	0
Indiana									
Volunteers of America of Indiana (VOA)	94	0	0	0	0	0	0	0	0
Kentucky									
Lee Adjustment Center (CORC)	770	1	0	0	1	0	0	0	0
Louisiana									
Allen Correctional Center (GEO)	1,450	0	0	0	0	1	0	1	0
Mississippi									
Delta Correctional Facility (CCA)	963	1	1	0	0	0	0	0	0
East Mississippi Correctional Facility (GEO)	858	1	0	1	0	0	0	0	0
New Jersey									
Hope Hall (VOA)	152	0	0	0	0	0	0	0	0
New Mexico									
Guadalupe County Correctional Facilty (GEO)[a]	591	0	0	0	0	/	/	/	/
Ohio									
Lake Erie Correctional Institution (MTC)[b,c]	1,428	5	0	5	0	0	0	0	0
Oklahoma									
Cimarron Correctional Facility (CCA)	952	0	0	0	0	0	0	0	0
Diamondback Correctional Facility (CCA)	1,892	0	0	0	0	0	0	0	0
Pennsylvania									
George W. Hill Correctional Facility (GEO)	1,919	0	0	0	0	0	0	0	0
Tennessee									
Hardeman County Correctional Center (CCA)	1,950	0	0	0	0	0	0	0	0
Metro Davidson County Deten-tion Facility (CCA)	1,077	3	3	0	0	0	0	0	0
South Central Correctional Center (CORC)	1,630	0	0	0	0	0	0	0	0

Appendix table 3a (continued). Allegations of inmate-on-inmate sexual violence reported in private prisons and jails, by type, 2005

Jurisdiction and facility	Average daily population, 2005	Reported inmate-on-inmate onconsensual sexual acts				Reported inmate-on-inmate abusive sexual contacts			
		Allega-tions	Sub-stantiated	Unsubstanti-ated	Unfounded	Allega-tions	Sub-stantiated	Unsub-stantiated	Unfounded
Texas									
Big Spring Community Cor. Center (Cornell)[a]	2,792	2	0	2	0	/	/	/	/
Bradshaw State Jail (CORC)	1,973	0	0	0	0	0	0	0	0
Bridgeport Pre-Parole Facility (CCA)[a]	196	0	0	0	0	/	/	/	/
Dawson State Jail (CCA)	2,166	2	0	1	1	0	0	0	0
Houston/Reid Community Cor. Facility (Cornell)	444	2	1	1	0	0	0	0	0
Limestone County Detention Center (CiviGenics)	762	0	0	0	0	0	0	0	0
Lockhart Pre-Parole Facility (GEO)	998	0	0	0	0	0	0	0	0
Mineral Wells Pre-Parole Facility (CCA)	2,030	0	0	0	0	0	0	0	0
Willacy County State Jail (CCA)	1,053	2	0	2	0	0	0	0	0
Virginia									
Lawrenceville Correctional Center (CCA)	1,568	0	0	0	0	0	0	0	0

Note: The total number of allegations includes ongoing investigations (not shown).
Abbreviations or acronyms of private corporations:
CCA - Corrections Corporation of America.
CiviGenics - CiviGenics Corporation.
Connections - The Connections Incorporated.
CORC - Corrections Corporation.
CSC - Correctional Services Corporation.
Cornell - Cornell Companies, Incorporated.
GEO - Global Expertise in Outsourcing.
MTC - Management and Training Corporation.
VOA - Volunteers of America.
/Not reported.
[a]Allegations of abusive sexual contacts could not be counted separately from allegations of nonconsensual sexual acts.
[b]Allegations limited to substantiated occurrences only.
[c]Allegations limited to completed acts only.

Appendix table 3b. Allegations of staff sexual misconduct with inmates reported in private prisons and jails, by type, 2005								
	Reported allegations of staff sexual misconduct with inmates				Reported allegations of staff sexual harassment of inmates			
	Allegations	Sub-stantiated	Unsub-stantiated	Unfounded	Allegations	Sub-stantiated	Unsub-stantiated	Unfounded
Total	29	6	18	5	7	0	7	0
Arizona								
Arizona State Prison-Kingman (MTC)	0	0	0	0	2	0	2	0
Central Arizona Detention Center (CCA)	0	0	0	0	0	0	0	0
California								
Central Valley Community Cor. (GEO)[a]	0	0	0	0	/	/	/	/
Taft Correctional Institution (GEO)	1	0	1	0	0	0	0	0
Colorado								
ComCor, Inc.[b]	0	0	0	0	0	0	0	0
Crowley County Correctional Facility (CSC)	0	0	0	0	0	0	0	0
Phoenix Center	0	0	0	0	0	0	0	0
Connecticut								
Cochegan House (Connections)	0	0	0	0	0	0	0	0
Florida								
Bay County Jail and Annex (CCA)	1	1	0	0	1	0	1	0
Moore Haven Correctional Facility (GEO)	0	0	0	0	0	0	0	0
South Bay Correctional Facility (GEO)	0	0	0	0	1	0	1	0
Georgia								
Wheeler Correctional Facility (CCA)[c]	/	/	/	/	/	/	/	/
Indiana								
Volunteers of America of Indiana (VOA)	0	0	0	0	0	0	0	0
Kentucky								
Lee Adjustment Center (CORC)	2	0	1	1	0	0	0	0
Louisiana								
Allen Correctional Center (GEO)	3	0	3	0	0	0	0	0
Mississippi								
Delta Correctional Facility (CCA)	0	0	0	0	0	0	0	0
East Mississippi Correctional Facility (GEO)[a]	3	0	1	2	/	/	/	/
New Jersey								
Hope Hall (VOA)	0	0	0	0	0	0	0	0
New Mexico								
Guadalupe County Correctional Facilty (GEO)	0	0	0	0	0	0	0	0
Ohio								
Lake Erie Correctional Institution (MTC)	0	0	0	0	0	0	0	0
Oklahoma								
Cimarron Correctional Facility (CCA)	0	0	0	0	0	0	0	0
Diamondback Correctional Facility (CCA)[a]	13	2	10	1	/	/	/	/
Pennsylvania								
George W. Hill Correctional Facility (GEO)[a]	1	1	0	0	/	/	/	/
Tennessee								
Hardeman County Correctional Center (CCA)	0	0	0	0	0	0	0	0
Metro Davidson County Detention Facility (CCA)	0	0	0	0	1	0	1	0
South Central Correctional Center (CORC)	0	0	0	0	0	0	0	0

Appendix table 3b (continued). Allegations of staff sexual misconduct with inmates reported in private prisons and jails, by type, 2005

	Reported allegations of staff sexual misconduct with inmates				Reported allegations of staff sexual harassment of inmates			
	Allegations	Sub-stantiated	Unsub-stantiated	Unfounded	Allegations	Sub-stantiated	Unsub-stantiated	Unfounded
Texas								
Big Spring Community Cor. Center (Cor-nell)[a]	2	0	2	0	/	/	/	/
Bradshaw State Jail (CORC)	1	1	0	0	0	0	0	0
Bridgeport Pre-Parole Facility (CCA)[a]	0	0	0	0	/	/	/	/
Dawson State Jail (CCA)[a]	1	0	0	1	/	/	/	/
Houston/Reid Community Cor. Facility (Cornell)	0	0	0	0	0	0	0	0
Limestone County Detention Center (CiviGenics)[a]	0	0	0	0	/	/	/	/
Lockhart Pre-Parole Facility (GEO)[c]	0	0	0	0	/	/	/	/
Mineral Wells Pre-Parole Facility (CCA)	0	0	0	0	0	0	0	0
Willacy County State Jail (CCA)	1	1	0	0	1	0	1	0
Virginia								
Lawrenceville Correctional Center (CCA)	0	0	0	0	1	0	1	0

Note: The total number of allegations includes ongoing investigations (not shown).
Abbreviations or acronyms of private corporations:
CCA - Corrections Corporation of America.
CiviGenics - CiviGenics Corporation.
Connections - The Connections Incorporated.
CORC - Corrections Corporation.
CSC - Correctional Services Corporation.
Cornell - Cornell Companies, Incorporated.
GEO - Global Expertise in Outsourcing.
MTC - Management and Training Corporation.
VOA - Volunteers of America.
/Not reported.

[a]Reports of staff sexual misconduct may include reports of staff sexual harassment.

[b]Reports of staff sexual misconduct are based on substantiated allegations only.

[c]Reports of staff sexual misconduct are not recorded in a central database.

Appendix table 4a. Allegations of inmate-on-inmate sexual violence reported in other correctional facilities, by type, 2005

Jurisdiction and facility	Average daily population, 2005	Reported inmate-on-inmate nonconsensual sexual acts				Reported inmate-on-inmate abusive sexual contacts			
		Allegations	Sub-stantiated	Unsub-stantiated	Unfounded	Allegations	Sub-stantiated	Unsub-stantiated	Unfounded
Total	9,547	2	0	0	2	1	1	0	0
U.S. Military									
Air Force	120	0	0	0	0	0	0	0	0
Army	1,113	0	0	0	0	0	0	0	0
Marines	631	0	0	0	0	0	0	0	0
Navy	730	0	0	0	0	1	1	0	0
U.S. Immigration and Customs Enforcement									
Aguadilla, PR*	5	0	0	0	0	/	/	/	/
Aurora, CO	15	0	0	0	0	0	0	0	0
Batavia, NY	454	0	0	0	0	0	0	0	0
El Centro, CA	480	0	0	0	0	0	0	0	0
Elizabeth, NJ	350	0	0	0	0	0	0	0	0
El Paso, TX	624	0	0	0	0	0	0	0	0
Florence, AZ*	343	0	0	0	0	/	/	/	/
Houston, TX	820	0	0	0	0	0	0	0	0
Laredo, TX	260	0	0	0	0	0	0	0	0
Los Fresnos, TX	600	0	0	0	0	0	0	0	0
Miami, FL*	580	0	0	0	0	/	/	/	/
San Diego, CA	1,119	0	0	0	0	0	0	0	0
San Pedro, CA*	393	0	0	0	0	/	/	/	/
Tacoma, WA	496	1	0	0	1	0	0	0	0
Jails in Indian Country									
Gila River Dept. of Cor. and Rehab., AZ	152	0	0	0	0	0	0	0	0
Hopi Rehabilitation Center, AZ	66	0	0	0	0	0	0	0	0
Red Lake Law Enforcement Services, MN	56	0	0	0	0	0	0	0	0
Rosebud Sioux Tribe Law Enforcement, SD	39	1	0	0	1	0	0	0	0
Supai Jail, AZ	11	0	0	0	0	0	0	0	0
White Mountain Apache Police Dept., AZ	65	0	0	0	0	0	0	0	0
Zuni Detention Facility, NM	25	0	0	0	0	0	0	0	0

Note: The total number of allegations includes ongoing investigations (not shown).
/Not reported.
*Allegations of abusive sexual contacts could not be counted separately from allegations of nonconsensual sexual acts.

Appendix table 4b. Allegations of staff sexual misconduct with inmates reported in other correctional facilities, by type, 2005

	Reported allegations of staff sexual misconduct with inmates				Reported allegations of staff sexual harassment of inmates			
	Allegations	Sub-stantiated	Unsub-stantiated	Unfounded	Allegations	Sub-stantiated	Unsub-stantiated	Unfounded
Total	14	4	4	5	5	2	1	1
U.S. Military								
Air Force	0	0	0	0	0	0	0	0
Army	2	0	1	1	0	0	0	0
Marines	3	0	0	3	0	0	0	0
Navy	2	1	1	0	0	0	0	0
U.S. Immigration and Customs Enforcement								
Aguadilla, PR*	0	0	0	0	/	/	/	/
Aurora, CO	0	0	0	0	0	0	0	0
Batavia, NY	0	0	0	0	0	0	0	0
El Centro, CA	0	0	0	0	0	0	0	0
Elizabeth, NJ	0	0	0	0	0	0	0	0
El Paso, TX	0	0	0	0	0	0	0	0
Florence, AZ	0	0	0	0	0	0	0	0
Houston, TX	0	0	0	0	0	0	0	0
Laredo, TX	0	0	0	0	0	0	0	0
Los Fresnos, TX	1	0	0	0	1	0	0	0
Miami, FL*	0	0	0	0	/	/	/	/
San Diego, CA	1	1	0	0	0	0	0	0
San Pedro, CA	0	0	0	0	0	0	0	0
Tacoma, WA	0	0	0	0	0	0	0	0
Jails in Indian Country								
Gila River Dept. of Cor. and Rehab., AZ	2	0	2	0	2	2	0	0
Hopi Rehabilitation Center, AZ	0	0	0	0	0	0	0	0
Red Lake Law Enforcement Services, MN	2	1	0	1	1	0	0	1
Rosebud Sioux Tr be Law Enforcement, SD	0	0	0	0	1	0	1	0
Supai Jail, AZ	0	0	0	0	0	0	0	0
White Mountain Apache Police Deprt., AZ	1	1	0	0	0	0	0	0
Zuni Detention Facility, NM	0	0	0	0	0	0	0	0

Note: The total number of allegations includes ongoing investigations (not shown).
/Not reported.
*Reports of staff sexual misconduct may include reports of staff sexual harassment.

www.ingramcontent.com/pod-product-compliance
Lightning Source LLC
Chambersburg PA
CBHW080740290526
45790CB00008B/3263